the bigmen

Personal memories of
Glasgow's police

Joe Pieri

Neil Wilson Publishing • Glasgow • Scotland

This book is dedicated to the memory of
Detective Superintendent Joe Beattie

First published by
Neil Wilson Publishing
303a The Pentagon Centre
36 Washington Street
GLASGOW
G3 8AZ
Tel: 0141-221-1117
Fax: 0141-221-5363
E-mail: info@nwp.sol.co.uk
http://www.nwp.co.uk

A catalogue record for this book is
available from the British Library.

ISBN 1-903238-07-2

Design by Mark Blackadder
Typeset in Ehrhardt

Printed and bound by ColourBooks Ltd, Dublin.

Contents

Acknowledgements

To the men on the beat who once patrolled the Hope Street beat and whose recollections have inspired this book.

To May Mitchell at the Strathclyde Police Museum in Pitt Street, Glasgow for helping me with much of the background information required for this book.

Preface

Once upon a time, at the top end of Hope Street, Glasgow, at the junction where it meets Renfrew Street (and where The Royal Scottish Academy Of Music and Drama now stands), there stood a blue police box.

Here, the men on the beat met at the change of shifts, filled in their journal and had direct communication with their headquarters in Maitland Street. Two paces away in the same street the Savoy café had one of its two entrances. The men on the beat found it much more comfortable to meet in the back shop of that establishment, rather than in the police box, for there they could stretch out at their ease and drink coffee, at the same time keeping their eye on the police box light in case of a call from the station. There was almost always a policeman in that back shop, from some beat or other, and the Savoy was jokingly named 'a substation of the Northern'. For four decades: the thirties, forties, fifties and sixties, there was hardly a 'polis' from the Northern who did not make use of the facilities of the Savoy and who was not known to the family who owned the shop. Friendships were formed which have lasted to this day, and the recollections of some of those beat men still alive, in conversation with me, the proprietor of the Savoy, form the basis of this book.

Joe Pieri, Lenzie,
September 2000

Beginnings

In 1800, after a bread riot in Glasgow which lasted for several days and could only be quashed with the help of the military, the decision was taken to establish a trained police force to maintain public order and to keep the streets safe for the people of the city. The control of this body was to be vested in the Provost, The Dean of Guild, and 24 elected commissioners, and the funding was to be provided by a tax imposed on all the citizens, taking the form of a tax on property which became know as the rates.

The members of this new force consisted of a chief, three sergeants, nine officers and about 70 watchmen to patrol the streets during the night. They were equipped with uniforms and greatcoats, staves and lanterns, and had more to do than just keep law and order. They also had to sweep the streets, and attend to the lighting and maintenance of street lamps. This force, although a big improvement on the old haphazard 'night watch', could not of course deal with large-scale disturbances, and often soldiers and cavalry had to be called in to help maintain order.

With a large population available to prey on, criminal gangs began to flourish. One of the most notorious of them was the infamous 'Penny Gang' which had about 300 members. On admittance to its ranks, each member had to pay a penny into a common fund and the money was used in the payment of any fines imposed by the authorities. These gangs extorted money from shopkeepers and traders, were noted for their extreme violence and the police had to be suitably equipped to confront them. One of the items of defence issued to the police was a thick leather neckpiece, similar in shape to a clerical collar, which protected them from having their throats slashed from behind.

The gangs also indulged in grave robbing for the purpose of clandestinely supplying bodies for anatomical studies, since in the early nineteenth century, because of religious taboos, it was forbidden to dissect bodies for any purpose. Much medical research was carried out on corpses stolen from their graves, and good money was on offer from medical students and institutions for a fresh corpse in good condition. In the case of the infamous duo, Burke and Hare, the bother of digging up graves was circumvented. They simply murdered their victim and sold the fresh body. Their principle customer was a Dr Knox, and he had to flee the country when their activities were unveiled. A children's street song of the day went as follows:

Doon the close and up the stair
In the hoose wi Burke and Hare
Burke's the butcher and Hare's the thief
Knox's the one who buys the beef

As the city increased in size by the incorporation of small neighbouring burghs such as Gorbals, Anderston and Calton, so grew the need for a larger and more integrated police organisation and by the late eighteen seventies the police force had grown to consist of over 1400 men under a chief constable and seven superintendents. The foundations for the development of the police in the next hundred years had now been laid. The main driving force behind the organisation of the police at this time was Chief Constable James Smart, the first man to carry the title. Under Smart's direction the Glasgow police force was to be moulded into a force for law and order which for organisation and efficiency was second to none.

It is interesting to note that a very large number of

these constables came from the Highlands and the Western Isles, and it is probable that by the end of the nineteenth century the 'Teuchters', as they were called, formed the largest group in the force. At the time of the Highland clearances, and the destruction of the traditional life pattern of the Highlands and Islands, many families came to the city in search of work, and the menfolk were ideally suited for service in the police.

The rapid growth of the city had brought about the building of tenement houses alongside factories, steel mills and docks to house the influx of settlers, who came mainly from Ireland and from the rural areas of Scotland. As this influx continued, these dwellings were packed to overflowing and in a short time had degenerated into noxious slums where people lived in Dickensian squalor. Such areas were breeding grounds for hooligans and criminals as well as the gangs which were beginning to give the city its terrible reputation. By the nineteen twenties the Gorbals had the Cumbies gang and the Beehive Mob, Bridgeton had the Billy Boys, Shettleston had the Baltic Fleet, Govan its Kelly Boys and Calton had the notorious Black Hand Gang.

These gangs were often split along religious lines and reflected the sectarianism which grew as the city expanded. Govan also had a gang called the Billy Boys (named after King William of Orange) and the Norman Conks, a south side gang made up of the Catholic hooligan element of the city, was their mortal enemy. Each of these gangs did their best to disrupt the other's frequent processions and marches through the streets, and this gave rise to violent clashes. Many of the gangs took part in criminal activities. The Beehive mob engaged in house-breaking and safe-cracking, and all extorted money from local shops and tradesmen who went in fear of having their premises wrecked if the demands of the gangs were not met. On Fridays and Saturdays, days when money

3

was usually available for the alcohol which bolstered up their aggressiveness, the gangs would sometimes roam the city in search of rival gangs to engage in battle and innocent bystanders could find themselves in the middle of frightening and prolonged street disturbances.

In 1924 mounted police were introduced to the city. The members of this new division were equipped with military type uniforms and sported sabres, most probably for ornamental purposes, as there is no known case of this weapon ever having been used. Until the early fifties their horses were stabled in a garage in Hill Street, opposite St Aloysius church.

These were very hard times for the police in Glasgow, and worrying times for the people of the city, who no longer felt it was safe to walk the streets. The situation called for drastic measures and in 1931, at a time when Glasgow had long since become notorious for its gangs and for its lawlessness, Percy Sillitoe was named Chief Constable of Glasgow. Before this appointment he was Chief Constable of Sheffield, where he had acquired a reputation for firmness and efficiency in dealing with the problems of that city, which were not very far removed from those which afflicted Glasgow. In his autobiography he makes this comment about the city:

> The city was over-run by gangs terrorising decent
> citizens and waging open war between themselves in
> the streets.

Sillitoe immediately proceeded to apply to the situation in Glasgow the same methods he had found so successful in Sheffield, and began ruthlessly and efficiently to break the power of the gangs. He picked the biggest, strongest and toughest men in the force, formed them into 'Heavy Squads', and gave them a completely free hand in using maximum force against street crime and hooliganism.

4

Depending on the size of the disturbance, about 50 or more of these 'Heavies' would be quickly transported in unmarked vans to the scene of a street fight, where they were unmerciful in their use of fist and baton against the brawling hooligans. The leaders of the gangs were often picked out for 'special' treatment. There was no such thing as a Council for Civil Liberties then, no complaints book as there is now in each police station and the punishment meted out by the police more than suited the crime. In a relatively short time Percy Sillitoe broke the power of the gangs by his tough methods, remaining as Chief Constable in Glasgow from 1931 to 1943. On retirement he was knighted for his services to the community.

Although the organised gangs were no longer active in the fifties and sixties, Sillitoe's no-nonsense, no-mercy methods were continued in the treatment of the casual hooligan and criminal. From his time on, woe betide any hooligan or 'ned', as they were called, who engaged in criminal activities or caused any trouble in the streets.

Although Sillitoe is mainly remembered by the public as the man who smashed the gangs, his impact on the Glasgow police was profound and far-reaching. He completely reorganised the force into one of the most progressive and innovative in the country. Until his arrival there was only one person who could deal with fingerprints, and any found at the scene of a crime had to be sent to Scotland Yard for comparison and identification. Under Sillitoe's direction a state of the art fingerprinting and photographic department was inaugurated and a forensic unit was set up. A radio station which permitted communication between HQ and the newly-introduced police cars came into being. Until late in the nineteenth century, the only wheeled form of transport, apart from the bicycle, that was available to the police was the 'Drunk Trolley'. This was a sort of wooden stretcher with leather restraints on wheels, which was used to transport the drunk and incapable to the nearest cells.

In order to rejuvenate the force Sillitoe enforced compulsory retirement for all officers after 30 years service. He formed an intelligence unit called 'C Specials' to investigate business fraud. This unit was instrumental in breaking up graft rings within the City Corporation. As a result of investigations no fewer than five city officials were sent to prison for corruption, one of whom was the convenor of the police committee.

So widespread was the dishonesty in the administration of Glasgow that in Sillitoe's autobiography it is stated that at one time Tom Johnson, The Secretary of State for Scotland, warned him that if the situation persisted it might become necessary to suspend the whole Corporation and to put in a Commissioner to run the city.

Sillitoe also employed women as telephonists, typists and clerks. Under his guidance the divisions were reorganised from 11 to 7, and the new ideas and procedures he introduced carried the Glasgow police forward until its incorporation into the larger Strathclyde Force in 1973.

This transition was carried out by Chief Constable McNee, who has the distinction of being the last Chief of the Glasgow Force and the first of the Strathclyde Regional Police Force. The organisational effort to bring about this change was enormous. The merging of seven different forces with different modes of practise presented great problems of harmonisation and that the transition was achieved successfully with a minimum of disruption is a measure of the skill and ability of the officers who carried it out.

The Northern

The Northern Division, with its headquarters in Maitland Street in the Cowcaddens, was one division created by Sillitoe. Because of its geographical location the problems encountered and dealt with by the Northern encapsulated every aspect of policing in the city.

Today, the Cowcaddens district of Glasgow is typical of a district in any modern European City. Criss-crossed by ramps leading to and from the M8 motorway, the district, immediately to the north of Glasgow City Centre, now consists of scores of ultra modern steel and glass buildings which serve mainly as offices and high-tech factories. The most imposing building in the district is the Glasgow Royal Concert Hall at the eastern end of Renfrew Street, which faces a high rise fortress-like car park and a well laid out bus depot at one of the slip-roads of the M8 motorway. No more than a block away from this magnificently structured edifice with its perfect acoustics, at the corner of Hope Street and Renfrew Street, the Royal Academy of Music and Drama dominates the scene. A few of the buildings of the old Cowcaddens still stand derelict, but these are being progressively demolished as development proceeds. The modern Cowcaddens is a model of what well thought out town planning can achieve, but half a century ago the reality was altogether different.

The Cowcaddens was then an area stretching from the north side of Sauchiehall Street to the canal banks in Port Dundas, and from the Buchanan Street goods railway station in the east to St Georges Road in the west. In it lived and worked as representative a cross-section of the population of the city as one could hope to see in one area. The vast goods-station alone, with its access to the Forth and Clyde canal at Port Dundas, employed hundreds of men from every social group. These men ranged from the administrative class down to the carters who manned the horse-drawn carts that reigned supreme until well into the thirties. They were used as a means for distributing goods throughout the city. The goods-station spread over 50 acres and on still, windless days an overpowering array of smells, composed of emanations from the stables and the variety of raw materials stored in the railway sheds lay like a miasma over the city. The large flow of goods passing through acted as a magnet for thieves and wrongdoers, who were dealt with by the railway's own police force, acting in conjunction with the men from the Northern.

On Garnethill there were houses and mansions, whilst at the other end of the scale, at the top end of Maitland Street and Milton Street, and in the mean streets along the Garscube Road slums could be found. Cowcaddens Street offered as great a variety of shops as the far more elegant Sauchiehall Street, running parallel one street removed to the south. These shops were certainly not as grand or as pretentious, but they offered more or less the same goods and services at a fraction of the price and many of the window-shoppers in the 'Sauchie' ended up a few hundred feet to the north, in the Cowcaddens, to make their purchases. Until the early nineteen thirties the two streets were joined by The Queens Arcade, a covered shopping area which led from the Cowcaddens at Stow Street through to Sauchiehall Street. At that end the shops were well appointed, as befitted their proximity to the famous thoroughfare, but as they approached the Cowcaddens end they became progressively more cheap and tawdry, in keeping with the appearance of the grimy tenements and the purchasing power of their inhabitants.

The area was awash with public houses and drinking dens of every description and quality. These pubs ranged from the squalid drinking dens of the Garscube Road, little better than shebeens and epitomised by the Jungle in neighbouring Milton Street, to the well appointed Atholl Arms in Renfield Street and the elegant Lauders in Sauchiehall Street. Lauders was at the southern fringe of the Cowcaddens, and had a richly embossed door and invitingly furnished interior. Garscube Road also sported a pub, imposingly named The Symposium, whose title and décor stood out like sore thumbs in the seedy surroundings. In Garscube Road alone there were 27 pubs to be found, and the Hope Street beat area of the Cowcaddens boasted 33 drinking places. Scattered throughout were numerous fish and chip shops and ice-cream cafés, whose appearance in the main reflected the squalor of the surrounding area. The fish and chip shops were invariably situated near large pubs. These guaranteed them a brisk trade, for pubs did not sell food in those days, and since they had to close at 9.30pm, the alcohol induced hunger of their customers could only be satisfied by a visit to the local 'Tally's'. The Cowcaddens proper boasted of one dance hall, the 'Tower Ballroom' in Garscube Road, a large echoing barn-like place which supplied the men on the beat with a never-ending stream of breach of the peace arrests.

Cinemas, or picture houses as they were more often called, proliferated, and one of them, The Green's Playhouse, on the opposite corner from the Pavilion Theatre, was the largest in Europe during the nineteen forties. There were two theatres, the up-market Theatre Royal at the top end of Hope Street, which staged plays and opera, and the more down-to-earth Pavilion in Renfrew Street, with its popular variety turns. A street width away across Sauchiehall Street stood The Empire Theatre of international fame. Over the years many of the large houses in the Garnethill area had been converted to small bed and breakfast boarding houses, and the many artistes who appeared regularly at the theatres had their lodgings there when visiting Glasgow, their presence adding an exotic and bohemian atmosphere to the district.

Illegal street bookies with their 'pitches' and runners abounded. Their clients added to the flow of assorted humanity on the streets. As a topping to this hotchpotch of activities there was the notorious Raven Club in Renfrew Court, an illegal gambling den which was a match in seediness and latent violence to anything that Soho had to offer.

The Cowcaddens was thus a melting pot of mixed activities and of different social groups, and was a happy hunting ground for the 'neds', prostitutes, thieves and assorted hooligans who plagued the district by day and night. It required policing of the very highest order to keep the cauldron from spilling over and the decent citizens protected, and this protection was more than adequately provided by the beat men who worked out of the Maitland Street police station.

Built at the south end of Maitland Street, almost on the corner of Cowcaddens Street, the station was a massive two storey granite-faced building with a frontage of about 200 feet. Flanked by two imposing Roman style columns on each side, the main entrance, two steps above pavement level, consisted of an arched doorway with heavy well-worn mahogany doors. Over the years these doors had acquired well-defined indentations at head height, formed by the use of recalcitrant prisoners' heads as door openers. Immediately on the right-hand side of the entrance there was the so-called 'bar', a long and wide polished wooden counter almost four feet in width, behind which stood the reception staff, composed of a turnkey, a bar officer and an inspector to deal with cases as they were brought in. At the end of the bar on the left there was an office staffed by a female turnkey whose job it was to deal with women prisoners and to take care of any lost children brought to the station. The female turnkey also saw to the serving of meals to the prisoners in the cells. These were simple affairs, consisting in the main of fries and sandwiches served with copious mugs of strong tea prepared in a small kitchen by women staff who doubled up as cleaners. It was also the female turnkey's duty to search women prisoners if the necessity arose, and the policeman in charge of one case involving women recounts the following:

One of the big clothes shops in Sauchiehall Street used to put a van on the road to sell clothing seconds round the housing schemes. It was a big van and it had six women in it to run things. These women got paid every Friday and one pay day they found that someone had nicked four pay-packets from the van. We were called in and it was obvious that the thief had to be one of them. So we brought them all in and gave them over to the turnkey to be searched. They were all gone over in her office, but she couldn't find a thing on any of them. So we put them all in the sergeant's room and called them out one by one for questioning. When one of them was walking towards us I noticed that she was walking a bit funny, and when she stood up to walk away after interrogation she seemed to be walking funnier still. So I called the female turnkey over and told her to take the woman into her office and to strip her down to the bare buff and search her naked. Well, she did, and did she not find all the money! The woman had taken all the notes out of the pay-packets and stuffed them up her privates. They were beginning to rub every time she moved and that was why she was walking so funny. That wasn't so bad though, at least those women were clean, more or less. You should have seen the state of some of them we brought in, absolutely manky. Everybody we brought in had to be searched, in case they had things on them that weren't allowed in the cells. They had to turn their pockets out themselves, but a lot tried to keep things back. Some of the modellers we brought in, usually for a breach or a drunk and disorderly, were in a filthy state and they were bad enough, hadn't washed for months, but nothing compared to some of the women, you could have got the plague from the smell of them, they were so bad. I wouldn't have had the female turnkey's job for a pension.

The cells, about 30 of them in all, were situated one level up from the bar area. During the war this section had been covered over with broad steel beams for protection against falling masonry in the event of a hit during an air raid. One level down were the toilets, a small office for the pay clerk, storage facilities and the equipment room. It was here that the night shift men were supplied with black helmet badges to replace the shiny metal ones sported during the day and here they were issued with their night lamps, heavy battery-powered contraptions, which had been on charge all day since the last night shift. They were bulky, cumbersome affairs and despite their powerful looking appearance the lamps were good only for short-range work. Most night shift men spurned their use, preferring to bring along their own torches, which could be hand held and also used as clubs should the need arise.

The backbone of the police force were the beat men, on whose shoulders the working of the whole system depended. They were the men who patrolled the pavements, watched over property, ever alert for wrongdoers, ever ready to deal with any accident or emergency. The Maitland station functioned with about 60 men serving three daily shifts in groups consisting of eight to ten men, each group with a sergeant. There was one inspector for 20 men. The early shift ran from seven in the morning to two in the afternoon, then another shift took over from 2 till 11pm and the night shift came on duty from 11pm till 7 am. The district was split up into beats, with one man allocated to each beat. These were laid out so that any two policemen were always within whistle earshot of each other, in theory at least, and able to meet regularly at prearranged places.

There were also three substations attached to the Maitland Street headquarters, one at St Rollox, one at Springburn and one at Millerston, all of them dependent on the Maitland station for their manpower. The housing schemes which were eventually to surround Glasgow as slum clearance areas were still to be built, so these outlying areas were sparsely populated and were patrolled by beat men on bicycles. All officers paraded at their divisional headquarters, in a muster-room, where they were briefed on events and given their duties for the day. The outlying beats had to be travelled to by public transport and the nearer ones on foot. The officers were allowed a half-hour meal break each day, which the men in the distant beats normally took sitting in their nearest police box, eating a piece which they had carried with them. Even the men on duty near their headquarters preferred to sit in the compar-ative comfort of a box for their break, for it gave them a full half hour for their meal, rather than use up part of it walking to and from their headquarters.

A much sought-after beat in the heavily populated areas near headquarters was the Hope Street beat. Because of the volume of activity in the area this beat was split into two sections, numbers six and seven, with two men in each section at all times . The beat had to be patrolled twice in the duration of each shift. On the night shift all shop and business premises had to be checked each time round and reports made from the police box to headquarters at designated periods. On the day shift, school crossings also had to be attended to by the man on the beat, and at busy traffic periods, main street intersections were controlled by a policeman on points duty. (Traffic lights did not make an appearance in Glasgow until the early fifties.) All these duties were, of course, interspersed with the many arrests and incidents that invariably interrupted the planned routine and which made it impossible sometimes to patrol the area as prescribed. This beat was the most desirable in the whole of the Cowcaddens. A policeman who served on that beat for more than 20 years tells why:

A cop's job on the night shift is a very lonely job. On the night shift you're walking on your own all the time, nobody to talk to. All you hear is the sound of your own boots on the cobbles and flagstones, you're checking up in dark dunnies and in back courts. The housebreakers don't go in from the front, they go in from the back, and that's where you have to check up on. A night shift on a beat up places like the Garscube Road was bloody awful. You've no idea what those slums were like, dark and dirty and smelly and everybody in them hates the polis. You can go the whole night without talking to a soul apart from your mate on the next beat when you meet up, and you can easily start imagining things. That's what was great about the Hope Street beat, it was really two beats in one, beats number six and seven it was. Beat six ran from Hope Street to Cambridge Street and beat seven went from Hope Street to Buchanan Street, so there were four men in those two areas. It was so busy you had to have a mate with you, because there was always something doing and if you ran a body into the station you could lose half an hour and you had school crossings and the Killermont bus station and things like that to think about. You had so many incidents on these two beats that a man alone on each one could never have coped, because there was always something doing. You were falling over cases every two minutes and you always had company. What made it busy too was the box at the Hope Street door of the Savoy, there was always some cop there phoning into headquarters and you could always nip into the back shop of the Savoy for a quick cup of tea. It must have been the busiest beat in the whole of Glasgow and you never wearied there. There was always plenty to do and there were some great characters around you could talk to. All the shopkeepers liked the polis there, we kept the neds away. Even on the night shift there was a lot doing and plenty of places you could go into for a smoke and a blether and a wee heat in the winter. But you had to know your business and you had to be able to handle yourself on a beat like that, because anything could turn up. Only the best out of the Northern got a permanent beat there.

Sixty years ago the only means of communication between policemen in a given area was by means of an Acme Thunderer, a heavy brass whistle used to summon help in a crisis situation. These whistles emitted a piercing blast, which in optimum conditions in the stillness of night could carry as far as 500 yards.

The man on the beat could make direct contact with his base only through the phone installed in the police boxes introduced by Percy Sillitoe some 15 years before, which were strategically situated every few hundred yards or so. Equipped with outside speakers which could be accessed by members of the public in case of emergency, these boxes were concrete structures resembling phone kiosks in shape, but much larger and able to accommodate three or four persons. On the roof was a light bulb, heavily protected by wire mesh, which flashed if the beat man was needed on the phone. The heavy wooden doors of some of the police boxes, especially in the rougher streets of the Cowcaddens, were distinguished by the same clearly defined indentations at head level as could be seen on the doors of the station and were caused by the same means.

On the inside, the boxes were equipped with a telephone and a journal into which the beat men had to enter their activities twice a day, with their next destination noted so that the sergeant would know exactly where they were. The discipline imposed on the man on the beat was strict, great emphasis was placed on writing up the journals so that all activity was well documented, and woe betide anyone found outside the area he was assigned to. Failure to detect a crime on a night shift would have to be explained to an irate superior, and many a night shift man has been called out of his bed during the following day to explain his failure in detecting a shop break-in during his shift. To avoid this, the old hands at the game lazed out the first part of a night shift and preserved their energy for the last couple of hours of duty. A burst of activity would then ensue, a thorough inspection of the beat would be done and any crime discovered would be reported.

One of these 'old hands' reminisces:

It was easy to miss a break-in on the night shift. The neds would be fly for you and knew every one of your moves. They'd wait until you'd checked a premises on your second round, give you ten minutes, then they would break into the place and the break-in wouldn't get discovered until the early shift man came in. That would get you a real telling-off from the bosses. So we got wise for that. We'd do a quick round of the beat at the beginning of the shift then hang around somewhere with some of the boys from neighbouring beats chewing the fat and things, then when the shift had an hour to go, you'd do a close inspection and report anything you found. As long as you filled in the journal when you had to and as long as you could see the box light in case you were needed you were OK. We had a young fella who was dead keen on the job and what he'd do when the rest of us were having a smoke, he'd go up to the first landing in a close and keep a watch on the backyards from the window. He called the backyards 'The ned's highway', 'cos that's where they walked with their loot after a job, they'd never walk on the pavement where they might be seen and he'd get a lot of good arrests that way. That way too he sometimes recovered the loot even before the break-in had been discovered!

One Saturday night, the two cops on the beat had a break-in at Da Prato's Italian delicatessen in Stow Street. One of the neighbours called the office to say that there were burglars in the shop downstairs and the two big yins get sent to investigate. They caught two neds in the shop red-handed, rifling the till and they grab them and took them up to the cells. Then they called Da Prato out and he got the door and the glass on the inside door fixed up and that was that. There was a firm called Hurry Brothers who came out any time to do emergency jobs. They made a fortune at weekends, the neds used to throw screw tops though shop windows for the fun of it, and that firm always came out quick to a call. Maybe that's why they were called Hurry. Well, anyhow, on Monday morning Da Prato opens up the shop as usual and after a while he hears a noise in the basement, so he goes down, and there's another ned, drunk as a skunk. The two polis hadn't searched the premises. They had assumed that the two they got were the only ones there, but there was one down below. He couldn't get out because the door had been sealed off, so he spent the weekend drinking his way through Da Prato's wine stock. The higher-ups don't like you to miss anything like that on a beat, so the two cops got a bollocking for not checking the premises properly.

The police boxes were also equipped with a well-stocked first aid box, a fire extinguisher and a water key. Burst pipes were frequent occurrences in the tenement houses, and the beat man was always handy when it came to turning off the water supply to a particular close should the need arise. The boxes were also used to lock up recalcitrant prisoners awaiting the arrival of a Black Maria, the name given to the plain black van used to transport prisoners to the cells in Maitland Street. The vans had no windows, the sole illumination was through two small wire-meshed glass apertures on the rear doors and two bench seats ran the length of the inside of the vehicle. These vans were also used for the quick transportation of policemen and carried a retractable steel ramp about 18 inches wide for use in the loading of motor bikes and bicycles.

On the night of 20 June 1940, the day Italy declared war on Britain, these Black Marias worked overtime carrying a quite different type of prisoner to the cells in Maitland Street. The cargo was load after load of Italians who had suddenly become enemy aliens and arrested that night for eventual transportation to internment camps by the military authorities.

One of the policemen who participated in the arrests tells this story:

We brought in over a hundred Italians that night. Some of them we knew from the beats we were on

18

and you couldn't help being sorry for some of them, leaving wives and kids behind, crying and all that. They were of all ages and shapes and sizes and the Northern was chock-a-block with them, packed it was, and we had to put them in tight, five and six to a cell until the military people could take charge of them. We had no room for any neds that night, so we arrested no one unless we absolutely had to, but one real bad bastard had to be hauled in. There was no room, so the only thing we could do was shove him into a cell with five Italians already in it. This bloke had stabbed another ned over a fight about some cigarettes they had looted from a smashed Italian shop [that night almost every Italian-owned shop in Glasgow was wrecked and looted by angry mobs] so we had to pull him in. So he finds himself locked up with five young guys he doesn't know are Tallys and he starts boasting about what he had done that night, and he nearly pisses himself with fright when he finds out who his cell mates were. He thought they were going to do him up so he starts screaming blue murder at the top of his voice and we had to take him out and lock him up in a downstairs storeroom on his own.

In 1966 a fire broke out in the Grandfare supermarket at the corner of Hope Street and Maitland Street and developed into a huge blaze, which destroyed the whole block. The store adjoined the police station, separated from it only by a narrow lane, and the blaze at one point threatened to spread to the police building. The prisoners in the cells had to be transferred to another station for their safety, but the efforts of scores of firemen managed to prevent the fire from spreading to the neighbouring building.

Some 20 years previously, in 1946, the station had survived another threat of destruction by fire. Katie Cameron who lived in the ground floor flat at 20 Maitland Street, directly opposite the main entrance to the police station, was doing the family wash in a large metal basin full of hot, soapy water. The working surface faced the window and her attention was caught by a group of youngsters pushing a barrow along the street. They lifted a large bundle of rags soaked in turpentine from the barrow, threw it down in front of the station doors, where it ignited, engulfing the wood in flames. Katie reacted quickly. She lifted the heavy basin, ran across the street and put out the fire with the soapy contents. The police reaction to the incident is not on record.

The Northern police station survived until the formation of the Strathclyde Force and the transfer of headquarters to its present position in Pitt Street in 1973, at which time the beat men vanished from the streets and their place was taken by the cruising panda car.

The building was then demolished to make way for the development of the new Cowcaddens, and a high-rise block of modern flats, one of the few in the Cowcaddens, now stands in its place.

The Big Men

The risks ran by the men on the beat were great and always present. Other jobs have their element of danger; fire-fighting, coal mining, North Sea oil work, etc, but the nature of the danger in these occupations is very different. The peril there is from the environment and from working conditions, whereas the police officer has a different kind of danger to confront in the course of his duty. There was always risk of attack from hooligans and criminals. Around every corner there could be danger, behind every door the possibility of assault and the officer on the beat was ever alert for such dangers.

During the war years, when many serving policemen of military age had joined the armed forces, men past military age and reservists who had come out of retirement made up the divisions. Whilst they were dedicated and courageous men, because of their age, they were often no match in speed and agility to the lawbreakers they sometimes had to tackle after an offence, but in the immediate postwar years these circumstances changed dramatically. The serving policemen who had gone to the armed forces resumed their prewar occupation – those who returned, that is, for many were killed in action – and they were joined by an influx of young recruits fresh from the battlefields of Asia, Europe and Africa. These men were highly trained and disciplined and in the peak of physical condition.

The minimum height requirement for the police was then five feet six inches. You would have been hard put in the nineteen fifties to find any beat man out of the Northern who stood under six feet in height, and many were a good three or four inches taller still. Add on another ten or so inches for their helmet and at seven feet tall their awesome appearance reflected the full authority of the law they were sworn to uphold. Almost all of these men had seen active service, many of them were skilled in unarmed combat and to men who had faced battle with a determined enemy, the neds and hooligans encountered regularly on some beats posed no problem whatsoever. The lawbreakers in these areas got the fright of their lives when they discovered that the men in uniform could run faster than they could, and twice the distance. When caught by them resisting arrest was futile. One of the men posted to a beat in the Cowcaddens recalls:

> It was my first time out on the beat alone in Cowcaddens Street and as I come round a corner, about 25 yards or so ahead I see two neds hanging around a shop window. A second-hand shop it was. One of them has a brick in his hand and throws it and smashes the window. They both grab something and start to run. I make up the 25 yards in no time and catch one, the other one was faster than his mate and had gone ahead, so I drag the one I'd got along by the sleeve and catch the first one too. They looked at me as though they couldn't believe it, they had never seen a polis run so fast in their lives.

The following are examples of the type of man who came on to the beat in the immediate postwar years:

Alex McGarvey of the Northern Division had joined the police the year before the outbreak of war, and in September 1939 enlisted in the RAF. He was a championship swimmer, a great friend of Willie Burns, the Scottish Champion, stood six feet in height and was immensely strong and powerful. After a period of training he was assigned to Lancasters as a pilot and flew scores of bombing raids over Germany.

His story is now told by a policeman colleague, a fellow pilot in the same squadron:

One day his Lancaster got hit by flak just off the coast of Holland and he was forced to ditch. Well, these big bombers had a valve, as soon as it hit the water it released a big rubber dinghy for the crew to get away in. His crew, bar one, got out, but these dinghies had one drawback, as soon as the wind hit them they would skoosh away a mile in no time. The one that didn't manage out was the navigator, he was wounded in the leg and couldn't move and McGarvey had to pull him out of his seat and drag him to the dinghy. But by the time he got there the dinghy had been carried away by the wind, and Alex was left alone with the wounded man on a sinking plane, so he blew up their Mae Wests and started swimming, pulling the wounded navigator. Well, I kid you not, 31 miles he floated and swam to the Dutch coast, 31 miles it was, towing a wounded man. They were about ten hours in the water when they got picked up nearly dead just off the shore by some Dutch fishermen. They didn't believe his story, how he had got there. They had to hand the two men over to the Germans and at first the Germans didn't believe him either, the story was so incredible, but they checked it out and so it was. He had swum 31 miles pulling a wounded man behind him. The Germans informed the Swiss Red Cross who told our people in London and he got a medal for it. He tholed out the rest of the war in a prison camp and the navigator survived.

The same officer recalls:

I joined the RAF just before the war in 1939. When war broke out I did my training for a while at Pensacola, the big American base. The Americans weren't in the war yet but a lot of our boys trained there just the same. From there we got sent to Dorval, near Montreal, then from there to Prince Edward Island in the Gulf of St Lawrence. There was a bloke there with us, Desmond White his name was. After the war he became the Celtic chairman. He was badly injured there, nearly copped his lot. A plane slipped its chocs and skidded into him, the prop hit his shoulder and nearly killed him. That's where he got his bad arm.

Then we did the U-boat patrols in the Gulf. We flew Catalinas there, up and down looking for U-boats. That was a bit hairy, we had to go up in all kinds of weather, I think maybe they were safer in the U-boats than we were up there. Went back to Nova Scotia then I got posted home. There I was teaching how to fly the beam. Every airfield had guidance beams, running down the main runway, they gave out a peeping signal and from it you could tell which side of the runway you were on. There was a beacon every five miles as you turn into the approach flight path, as you turn in the sound keeps you right. Crude compared to what we have now, but state of the art then. Then I was shifted to piloting Flying Fortresses. I saw a fair bit of active service along the Norwegian coast as far down as the coast of Holland and did a bit of bombing here and there. I really only had one hairy experience. One day we're coming back from a raid and we get well blootered by flak and the plane starts juddering all over the place. After a while the tail gunner Lofty comes up to the cockpit and says:

'Hey, there's a bloody great hole back there.'

I can tell something's wrong with the tail because I can't keep the plane straight and everything's shaking like mad, but to keep everything calm I tell him to go back to the turret and not to worry, everything's OK, and that we'll be back at base soon. We're near the runway now and the plane is shaking and shuddering all over the place, so I tell one of the crew: 'go back and tell Lofty to come forward in case the tail breaks off', and the guy comes back and says 'Lofty's no there, there's just a bloody big hole.' 'Lofty's no there?' says I, 'well, he must have forgotten about the hole and fell out'.

As I'm getting ready to land I get a diversion. If you were knocked up you were diverted to another airfield or runway in case you mucked up the runway for the rest of the in-coming aircraft and as I'm approaching the emergency field with the plane shaking something awful with hardly any control, I get another message from the ground.

'You've got something hanging out of a hole in the back. Christ! It's a body!'

So we just manage to pull Lofty up before we hit ground and the tail breaks off. I really thought we had all copped our lot that time. Lofty finished up OK, a wee bit bashed about and a wee bit of frostbite here and there, but nothing special. He joined the London Met as soon as he got demobbed.

I was demobbed in 1946 and since jobs weren't easy to get I decided to join the police. I trained at Oxford Street and then I was posted to the Northern in

Maitland Street, where it all started off. A lot of guys from the RAF joined the polis then.

Another man who arrived at the Northern at that time was John ——, 'Big John' as he was to be known for the next 29 years. At the age of 78 he still stands erect and strong at six feet three in height. He served during the war in the Royal Navy and tells his own story:

> I joined the Navy straight from my job as a fisherman sailing out of Wick, where I was born, and when the war came I wanted to see some adventure so I joined up. I was 18 at the time. I helped a bit to evacuate the soldiers at Dunkirk from a destroyer and then I volunteered for Special Forces. We were trained in underwater stuff, you know the kind of thing, checking boats for limpet mines in the Med, underwater demolition and stuff like that. The Italians were using two man subs to stick mines onto our ships in Gibraltar, they sunk one or two that way and when we got wise to how they were doing it we kept an underwater watch and knocked a few of them off before they could get to their target. We couldn't stop them with grenades or depth charges when they were near our ships. That might have set off their mines and sunk us.
> Then we went to underwater demolition, to demolish barriers just off beaches, you know the kind of thing, steel rails and barbed wire and all sorts of junk like that sunk in the water to rip the bottom off landing craft and snag up the soldiers coming off and trying to wade on to shore. We saw a bit of action at Pantelleria and Sicily and at the Anzio landings then we got posted back to Portsmouth. A

couple of days before the invasion, we got our orders and we came off a sub just off the beach in Normandy, 15 of us. We were loaded up with limpet mines. We had some strapped round us and some we were pushing ahead of us on inflated belts loaded with them and we had to stick them on to the barricades under the surface. These mines were timed, nobody knew when they were set to go off apart from the boys in London. The reason why they were timed was that when they went off the Germans would know that something was on and they would get ready. After the mines were set, and that wasn't an easy job either, under the water with the barbed wire and iron rails and things, we couldn't go back to the sub. We had just shorts on and flippers and we had to swim ashore.

When we got there the French resistance people were waiting for us. We had special wristbands for identification, just like a wristwatch but with a copper medal in place of the watch. The medal had the head of a French soldier on it and some writing in French, and that way they knew who we were. Come to think of it those wristbands must be something special now, there must be only 15 of them in the world. We went with the Maquis and they fitted us out with clothes and guns and grenades for another job we had to do. The night before the invasion started the Maquis got a signal from London. We had to kill as many German officers as we could that night, not soldiers, just officers, so as to break the chain of command for the invasion starting. The Maquis knew where they all hung out, bars and restaurants and brothels and places like that and during that night we burst in on

27

them and killed a lot. It was a lousy, dirty way to kill a man, when he's sleeping and not expecting it. It's different when you're in a battle, you're facing somebody who can fight back, but lousy or not we had our orders and it had to be done. It didn't bother the Maquis, though, they hated the Jerries in a way that we didn't, the Jerries had taken their land and their women and they took a great delight in killing them that way. When the invasion started we helped the Maquis to sabotage things, blowing up railway lines and mining roads and stuff like that. It was a bit hairy, because we didn't know what was happening on the beaches and we didn't know how we would end up or whether we would see our own lads again We weren't half relieved when our boys finally did break through and we could join up with them.

That was the type of man who appeared on the beats of the Northern division in the late forties and early fifties. That was the type of man sent out to deal with the petty criminals, thieves and razor-slashers who plagued the Cowcaddens. And deal with them they did.

Until the opening of the modern police training college in Tullieallan in the early sixties, recruits received their training in the centre in Oxford Street and then later at Polkemmet Castle in West Lothian. There they were taught the basic skills of the policeman. The training was hard and intensive and some who came directly out of civilian life dropped out early in the programme, unable or unwilling to maintain the high standard required. Physical fitness was essential. All police procedures had to be learned by the recruit. Laws and by-laws were explained and the basics set to memory for application in situations to be encountered on the beat. Lifesaving and first aid techniques in all environments had to be practised, swimming had to be mastered and driving skills acquired on a skid pan close to the training centre. After some months of training the recruit would then be assigned to experienced constables so they could see how the job was actually done, after which, having gained some experience, he would be left on his own. By this time he would have been issued with a small booklet: *Aide Mémoire for Constables* which set out a long and detailed list of contraventions likely to be encountered by the officer in the course of his duties.

The two years from the end of training would be reckoned as a probationary period, at the end of which the recruit could be dismissed without explanation. During this time, the recruit would be assigned to a division where he performed relieving duties, standing in for officers on holiday or on sick leave. His activities were well supervised by his superiors, any special abilities were duly noted and then his police career would begin, usually by assignation to a beat. The type of beat given would be matched to the new man's abilities and if the beat assigned happened to be a busy one offering a varied background of activities that was cause for satisfaction. City centre beats were much prized, as were those that touched on the city centre. Most hated were the slum beats, the Gorbals, the Garngad, the Saracen, the Garscube Road, with their row upon row of depressing and squalid tenements. The grime and dereliction of these places is difficult to convey in words, and those of the younger generations who have never seen such places and who have had the good fortune never to have lived in one might find it hard to appreciate the grimness and squalor that reigned there. It was in these areas that the notorious Glasgow gangs reigned and where prostitution, protection rackets and drinking dens flourished. Relative to the population, more murders were committed in Glasgow in those days than anywhere else in Scotland, and most of them were committed in and around the slum areas. Such areas, understandably, were not popular with the men who had to patrol them. In better class districts the beat policeman was the friend. In the slum areas he was the enemy. One instructor with an off-beat sense of humour always started his lectures with this remark:

'Now, remember, when you get on the beat, your best friend there is the ned. Without him you wouldn't have a job!'

That type of policing needed a high degree of physical courage and brawn. Courage and physical strength were required when going into a pub to break up a fight, in the sure knowledge that knives and razors were being used, and were just as likely to be used against the policeman as against anyone else. Courage and physical strength were needed to go into a neighbourhood to arrest someone in the sure knowledge that perhaps a hostile crowd had to be faced down in the process, and courage was needed to patrol a beat at night in the Garngad and Garscube Road pavements in the knowledge that an attack could come unexpectedly out of the night.

Appropriate methods were used to deal with trouble-makers. There was no mention in those days about civil rights and the careful treatment of offenders. Although the 'Heavy Squads' no longer existed in the forties and fifties and the men who had served in them were approaching retirement age, the philosophy of Percy Sillitoe still lived on. If someone fell foul of the law and resisted arrest or attempted to assault the policeman, then they had to take the consequences. A crack on the head, or, more painful, a crack on the ankles with a baton, and the promise of more to come, was enough to tranquilise even the most recalcitrant of prisoners.

Crime in those days was relatively uncomplicated, but very violent. Murders and deaths by violence were in the main confined to the slum areas, though when one did happen it would be headline news for days on end. Nowadays it seems that unless a murder is a spectacular multiple affair with sexual overtones it barely merits a few newspaper paragraphs. Breaches of the peace and housebreaking were the most common offences. There was little, if any, car theft (there were very few private cars on the road then) vandalism was rare, but armed robbery was not uncommon, and safe breaking was a popular occupation amongst criminals. In the years immediately after the war explosives were easily obtained and safes were broken into by simply blowing them open.

All this, together with the occasional gang battle and street disturbance, the frequent breach of the peace in public places and domestic violence incidents, just about made up the spectrum of crime in Glasgow in those far-off days.

There was hardly a beat man in the Northern who at one time or other had not been stabbed or wounded in the course of his career. Disturbances in the form of fighting in the streets after pub closing time were a regular Friday and Saturday night occurrence and any policeman who intervened was just as liable to be injured as the actual participants in the fracas. Pitched battles between rival football fans at matches were weekly occurrences, especially at games between Celtic and Rangers where the religious polarisation of the supporters invariably erupted into violence. It is a reflection on the expectation of violent confrontation at these games when senior police officials could claim that matters had gone off peacefully with such statements as 'there were only 50 arrests'. Some breaches of the peace and other minor disturbances were very often dealt with summarily on the spot by the beat men. A firm cuff around the ears and the offending hooligans would be sent on their way, for the cells in Maitland Street would have been filled to overflowing at the weekends had the strict letter of the law been adhered to in respect of incidents of assault and breach of the peace.

The ex-Royal Navy man quoted earlier, who joined the force after being demobbed, reminisces:

After the war I didn't want to go back to fishing so I joined the Glasgow police in 1946 right out of the Navy and went for training. After what we had learned in the Navy, police training was a skoosh. When I finished that, I was posted to the Northern in Maitland Street. The Cowcaddens might have been a real rough area but it was like a convent compared to what came next. Big Davy ——— and I started there on the Hope Street beat as rookies and we had an older man to show us the ropes, to show us how things were done on the beat. Inspector Fenton was in charge in the Northern at the time and after a few weeks he told us, 'Look, your probation's not even half started but I like the way you two do things and the way you handle yourselves out there. I've got an area that needs cleaning up, the Saracen, and I think that you two can do it. You two can manage no bother with the neds, and if you do all right in the Saracen you'll get a permanent beat right away.'

Now, you don't normally get a beat right away, you've usually got to wait a bit, and to get offered a beat just like that, well! I'm telling you, to get a beat is great. It's better than anything if you're a rookie. That beat's yours, you've to look after it, you're responsible. You're the man in charge of keeping the peace. In training you're told your job is to protect life and property and your beat is the place you're going to do it in. You're the man people come to for help. You're the man who has to sort things out. You've been accepted. Because you see, at the end of two years probation you can get sacked, no reason given, no warning, you're just told you're not suited for the job and you're out. And we only had a couple of months' service in and we got told we would get a beat! That was really something, so we were gonny do our best. So we went up to the Saracen with a couple of older men to show us around the place and then we were left on our own to get on with it. The Saracen was dreadful. Guys were getting demobbed, the area had nothing in it except tenements, streets and streets of tenements, the worst slums you ever saw, with just Saracen Street running through it with pubs and shops. These pubs and shops used to get wrecked if they didn't give the neds something. The guys who came back had done the war, they had had a rough time, they didn't want to pay for anything, especially whisky: pay for whisky, no way, pay for fags, no way. So they went into pubs at the demand and if they didn't get what they wanted they wrecked the place. The same in Tally shops: we won the war, pay for fish and chips: no way.

You, as a cop, were supposed to protect the public and we did just that. We sorted the neds out. No mercy, pick out the biggest of them, pick out the leaders, hit them hard and give them a good tanking and show them who was boss. If anybody caused trouble anywhere on our beat we would find out who they were and we'd go after them, even for days, until we got them. When we did we showed no mercy, we gave them a tanking they'd never forget and made sure they knew what it was for. We didn't bother to run many of them in, unless it was for something really bad, a slashing or a stabbing or something like that. For anything less they'd only get fined a few quid, and then they'd get it back at the demand from the shopkeepers and traders, but after we had finished with them you can bet they never bothered anyone again. We were fair and dead straight, we never did anyone who didn't deserve it and we never messed anybody about who didn't need messing and everybody knew that after a while. Davy and I got known as the Wolf Men there, the neds scarpered when we appeared and after a few months the Saracen was a peaceful place. To be known as the Wolf Men, that was good for us, everybody respected us and we could walk the beat with a wee swagger. The decent people thought we were great, they weren't all bad there, and the shopkeepers couldn't thank us enough, they didn't get bothered now.

We were there for six months and Fenton kept his word and right away we got the Hope Street beat in the Cowcaddens. The Hope Street beat! That was the best beat in the whole of Glasgow and Davy and I got it and after only about a year in the force! The Cowcaddens was great, it was a rest after the Saracen. Every day there was Christmas day after the Saracen. And the great thing, we were accepted by other police. When you're a young cop you had to know your place. You couldn't take another man's seat, you had to know your place in the station, but we made our mark right away and we were accepted, and not even after a year!

Gambling

In the days when each high street did not boast its quota of plush betting shops as it does now, the illegal street bookie was a well-known part of the city scene and a certain amount of time had to be given by the beat man to the observance of their activities and the comings and goings of their customers. The chance of easy money attracts criminals like honey attracts a bee, and since money flowed freely from the public into the pockets of the bookie, the hooks and crooks were always around to see if any of that flow could be directed into their own pockets. Moreover, many thieves liked a flutter on the horses, and any increase in the cash flow from any particular punter might indicate that ill-gotten money was being thrown at the events on the racetrack, and such information was always very useful in the investigation of a particular crime.

The average punter who wanted a shilling flutter on the dogs and horses had no option but to make use of the services of the illegal street bookie. Cash betting, except on the actual racecourse, was illegal, and the vast majority of the betting population were not creditworthy enough to indulge in the luxury of a postal or phone bet with the accredited firms of bookies, who went by the grandiose title of 'Turf Accountants'. Nor was it possible in the main for them to visit the racecourse to place a bet, therefore the illegal street bookie and his 'Pitch' flourished. The same strictures did not apply to the punter's attendance at dog-racing, for there were several dog-racing tracks within a tuppeny tram ride of the city centre. These were always packed on racing nights and the bookie could operate quite legally within the confines of the stadium.

The Hope Street beat had more than its fair share of

these pitches, ranging from the well run Joe Docherty's in Wemyss Street to the smaller and less pretentious pitches in the back streets and lanes. Some of these bookies were colourful characters. Joe Docherty always dressed impeccably, was well spoken when he wanted to be, and could well have been at home on the floor of a stock exchange. Laurie Ventre of the Garscube Road, who was of Italian extraction, was a flamboyant extrovert who had the reputation of being the Robin Hood of the district, ready to help anyone in need. Countless stories were told of his generosity to old people in need at a time when there was no social security system to take care of those unable to buy life's basics. When he died in the mid-sixties his funeral rivalled that of any Chicago godfather. He came from a long line of bookies: the records show that in 1917 a Mary Ventre was charged with having some betting slips and the sum of £6 in her possession.

Robert Boni, also of Italian origin, had a pitch in Ferguson Lane and had the reputation of being fair and dead straight in his dealings. He was a fearsome fighter who had no need of 'hard men' amongst his runners, he himself was more than capable of handling whatever aggravation might come his way and predators knew better than to give him any trouble.

Equal in size to Joe Docherty's operation, though perhaps not in quality of customer, was Jimmy Bell's in the Cowcaddens, inherited from his mother, the legendary 'Ma' Bell of the early thirties. Jimmy Bell was a true entrepreneur, for his interests included a range of flats in the imposing Charing Cross Mansions at Charing Cross and the prestigious 'Piccadilly Club' in Sauchiehall Street. Situated on the top floor of a building next to Lauders pub, the Piccadilly was the only nightclub in Glasgow. Luxurious, it featured the best in dance band music and cabaret and was frequented by the cream of Glasgow and visiting society. It was also well patronised by many town councillors and other influential persons and the whisper, never substantiated, was that no proper license had ever been issued for the club, but that it was allowed to operate on the sufferance of the powers that be. Jimmy Bell was also a fine musician. In his youth he had played the saxophone in the Louis Freeman band of Plaza fame and when the fancy took him he would join the orchestra on the podium at the Piccadilly club for an hour's performance on the sax.

It has to be remembered that in those days there were very strict laws governing public houses and places of entertainment and everything closed down tight on a Sunday in Scotland. Those were the days of the 'bona fide traveller', when anyone wishing to partake of alcoholic beverages could take a tuppenny tram drive out to Milngavie or some such outlying district. There a drink could be had at the local inn by signing a register to the effect that you were a traveller at the time of the purchase and you could then proceed to drink yourself blind. No pub, cinema or any kind of entertainment venue was allowed to open on the Sabbath and even innocuous ice-cream cafés selling nothing more pernicious than a plate of hot peas, raspberry-topped MacCallums and a cup of Bovril had to close at eight o'clock. In defiance of this last law, a café owner name of Persichini opened his premises, at the corner of Union Street and Argyle Street, every Sunday without fail, until midnight. On each of those nights after eight o'clock the café was duly visited by the police, who would gravely inform the owner that he was in breach of the law. He would then be charged and summoned to appear in front of the magistrate the following morning, where he would regularly pay a two pound fine, all done with appropriately dramatic flourishes. This procedure carried on for years until the outbreak of war, when the offending Persichini was put away on the Isle of Man as an enemy alien for the duration.

All the bookies' pitches ran amicably side by side, no

one poached on another's territory, and they were guarded by their runners, who protected their employer against any form of interloper, be it gangs bent on extortion or the police bent on enforcing the law. The runners also served as bet collectors, for not only was it illegal for these street bookies to operate, but it was also against the law for any citizen to make cash bets with them. Any punters found on the bookies' premises during a police raid could be arrested and fined, so in order to avoid this risk many clients stayed away and placed their bets directly with the runners.

A detective who participated in many such raids recalls:

> We used to keep a list of all the local bookies in the division headquarters with a row of dates marked on them. These dates marked the various days on which the bookie in question had been raided, and the officer in charge did his best to make sure that each bookie was raided an equal number of times in any given period. During quiet times when we didn't have too much to do the Super ran his finger down the list and picked the bookie who was to get done the next day. We did the raids always in the same way. It depended on the size of the pitch and on how many we expected to arrest. Maybe a dozen of us, plain-clothes and uniformed, we would barge in with Black Marias and seal off the pitch. Everyone there got nicked and taken in the vans to the station where they got charged. There was never any trouble. Everybody took it as a big joke.

The bookie's fine was usually in the order of £20 or so, and each punter would be fined a pound or two, the amount depending on the perceived financial standing of the punter as suggested to the presiding magistrate by his manner of dress and demeanor. This fine was always paid by the bookie, and moreover, to compensate for the inconvenience and indignity of arrest, each punter was presented with a couple of pounds to mollify his injured feelings. More often than not, the whisper of an impending raid would seep down to the bookie in question. Since punters did not take kindly to being arrested and spending a few hours in the cells, and since the bookies believed in looking after their customers, regular clients woud be warned off and the premises filled with the inhabitants of the local model lodging house. These down-and-outs would queue up very happily for the privilege of having themselves arrested, for on release they would pocket a pound tip from the bookie plus the treat of a fish supper at the local 'Tally's' for their trouble. Some bookies were better connected than others in receiving whispers of impending raids, for on those occasions their premises seemed always to have old winos and modellers as customers and no one else.

By and large the street bookies were reasonably law-abiding citizens well regarded and tolerated by the police. Severe sentences and very heavy fines would have soon put them all out of business, but their existence did no harm, they were a valuable source of information as to cash flow and movement among the criminals, and indeed it could be argued that their existence served a general public desire.

When the need arose, however, the police could act swiftly and decisively against any particular pitch. Another policeman remembers:

> There was a real bad pitch just off the Garscube Road. It was run by a fella called 'Biaj', Tony Biagi his real name was. A lot of low life hung around

there, and we knew for a long time that the pitch was used for reset and that Biaj was a fence. We raided the place and found a mass of stolen stuff. We went in heavy-handed, we expected trouble from the neds there but nobody lifted a finger to us. They all knew what they would have got if they had.

The raid resulted in Tony Biagi's conviction for reset and in his deportation to Italy, the land of his birth. Arrested in that raid were two other shady characters of Italian origin, one Victor Russo, who habitually carried an unloaded six-gun in his belt and who had the reputation of being a somewhat harmless nutcase with delusions of toughness, and a certain Goldie Coia, a fraudster and bank robber who regularly hit the headlines in spectacular fashion. Harmless he may have been, but Victor Russo was the bane of the beat man and of the magistrates, to whom he caused endless trouble. He was arrested repeatedly on charges of disorderly conduct and once, in the course of 12 days, he appeared in court no less than five times. The exasperated authorities attempted to raise a deportation order against Russo, but they failed, since he was Glasgow born and therefore a British subject.

Goldie Coia was a remarkable man with a great deal of talent who could have achieved much had he kept to the straight and narrow. He was brought up in Belshill where his father ran an ice-cream shop. There, as a boy, he was involved in a tragic accident. When about ten years of age, he was on a visit with his parents to his uncle and in a desk drawer he discovered what he thought was a toy pistol. He pointed it at his uncle in jest, pulled the trigger and killed him with a bullet in the eye. What the boy thought was a toy was in fact an only too real and fully loaded automatic pistol.

In his late teens Goldie embarked on a life of fraud and crime, his first exploit being the hold-up of a bank in Renfield

Street in the late thirties. He walked into the premises and pointed a napkin-covered finger at a teller and demanded money. The teller had no way of knowing that there was no gun under the napkin, only a finger, so he duly handed over a bundle of banknotes. With his newly gained wealth Goldie went to the downstairs washrooms in the Central Station, treated himself to a haircut and a shoeshine and tipped the boy £5! That was much more than a week's wages then and the bemused shoeshine went immediately round the corner to the Horseshoe Bar in Drury Lane and stood everybody there drinks. This very unusual largesse filtered down to the attention of the police, who had no difficulty in tracing it back to Goldie, who got a jail sentence for his pains.

On his release he never looked back and embarked on a lifetime career of fraud and deceit in nearly every country in Europe, where he spent a fair amount of time in jail. He never again, however, used violence or the threat of violence in his escapades. His death some years ago was the occasion of an article in the *Daily Record* which gave a brief résumé of some of his more spectacular exploits. Once, and this exploit is not mentioned in that article, with the help of some friends in the crew of *The Queen Mary*, which was at the time on a regular transatlantic route, he smuggled himself aboard the liner and hid in the crew's quarters. He emerged each day to circulate with the paying passengers and became one of the best known faces in the first class section. At the end of the journey he was several hundred pounds the richer, money legitimately won from passengers at the card tables. His deception was uncovered on arrival in the USA by the immigration author-ities, and he was immediately shipped back to the UK in the same liner, this time well under guard in steerage. At the time of his death he was negotiating with the *Record* for the right to write the story of his life of crime. At the beginning of Goldie's career in crime a deportation order was also made against him, but that too failed, since he, like Russo, was British born.

A deportation order which did not fail was one brought against a certain Serafina Rigardo who ran a notorious shebeen-cum-gambling-house-cum-brothel in Argyle Street at Anderston Cross. This house was open literally 24 hours a day for the purposes of drinking outwith permitted hours, all sorts of gambling activities, and for sexual favours. Although well and discreetly run for an establishment of its type, the constant stream of visitors and taxis at all hours of the day and night gave rise to repeated complaints on the part of Serafina's neighbours, which resulted in a protracted police surveillance on the flat. It is not as easy as it may seem to prove that a house is being run as a shebeen. The fact that dozens of people are sitting around in a room quaffing whisky after whisky is not enough. They may, after all, be guests at a party and it must be shown that substantial amounts of liquor are stored on the premises and that money is being paid for the liquor consumed before action can be taken. Finally, after a protracted surveillance, a full-scale raid netted almost 50 gallons of alcohol in the form of spirits and wines on the premises, plus a dozen or so females known to the police as prostitutes. Serafina was charged with 'trafficking in liquor without possessing a license', fined £100 and when it was discovered that she was an Italian citizen, immediately deported. It is surprising to note that the number of people of Italian origin in, and on the fringes of, the underworld was fairly numerous, given that the Italian colony in Scotland at that time was only a fraction of what it is now.

Joe Docherty's brother Sam also had a pitch in the neighbourhood. His one claim to fame was the famous Royal Bank of Scotland case of the early sixties. One Monday morning two of Sam's runners presented themselves at the Cowcaddens Street branch of the bank with a sum of money to be deposited in Sam's account. One of them wrote out a deposit slip, the teller checked the cash and gave the runner a receipted counterfoil for the amount deposited. That amount was £9,995, a very large sum for those days, but the teller had failed to notice that on his receipt the amount had inadvertently been set down as £90,995, a mistake of one zero digit. Sam was not slow in noticing this, and when his monthly statement came in from the bank, he decided to chance his arm and proceeded to ask indignantly as to why his statement was £81,000 short, producing the receipt as proof of the bank's mistake. The bank quite properly contested that the affair was simply a teller's error in misreading the sum written on the deposit slip, and that no such massive sum as £90,995 had ever been deposited.

With the help of a lawyer who seemed to think that Sam had a case, the bank was taken to court in an attempt to retrieve the allegedly missing £81,000. The case became the cause célèbre of its day. A succession of hooks and crooks proceeded to perjure themselves on Sam's behalf, but their testimony was contradictory and unconvincing, and when it became plain that such a sum, in five pound notes as claimed, would have required several large suitcases for transportation, the presiding Judge, Lord Cameron, threw the case out of court. The Lord was scathing in his remarks to the pursuer, making it plain to him that he ought to be charged with attempted fraud and his witnesses with perjury.

The unabashed Sam quite legitimately argued that he was only asking that the bank honour its receipt and nothing else and escaped prosecution. The affair did not endear Sam to his brother, for the publicity had done the family name no good whatsoever. The older and honest brother Joe believed in the principle that if you were trying to be a fly man you had to be a reasonably honest fly man, and not an obvious rascal.

43

Sam went on in later years to become a successful boxing promoter and staged several championship bouts in a Glasgow stadium.

*　　　　　*　　　　　*

Some forms of gambling were not tolerated, purely because they disturbed decent people and often gave rise to pitched battles in the street between the participants. In the dingy back yards and derelict vacant spaces of the Cowcaddens 'Pitch and Toss' schools were regularly organised by the local neds. At these venues, which were frequented by local hooligans for whom betting on horses did not provide enough excitement, half crown pieces were pitched at a target placed on the ground. The winner, who collected all the money thrown, was the one nearest the target. These were rowdy and noisy affairs, which more often than not ended up in a fracas. They definitely 'breached the peace' and were broken up immediately they came to the notice of the men on the beat.

One of these men tells:

You had to be strong to tackle some of those neds. I remember two, Foy and O'Hara. They called themselves the Kings of the Garscube Road. O'Hara was a short, tough man built like the side of a house. He was a belt man. The belt man's job was to stand next to the money at the pitch and toss schools with a brass buckled leather belt in his hand. He used it to keep away anybody who tried to pinch anything off the ground. A crack on the head from the brass buckle and you were a stretcher case right away.

Funny how things come back to you. The two used to run a pitch and toss school on a bit of vacant ground just off the Garscube Road on a Sunday afternoon. It was against the law and we used to run them in quite often, once a month or so or when we got complaints, which was nearly always. The neds who tossed there nearly all got drunk and made a terrible noise and there were constant fights amongst them. The neighbours were never done complaining. There was a chapel at the side of the vacant ground, and we used to go up to the priest's house, Father Gallagher I think his name was, so we could see who was down there, and we would take note of their names.

Then we would come down and rush in and say, 'you're all done, you and you, and you, and you'. Usually these pitch and tossers never gave you much trouble, but one day, I can't remember the reason why, there was a bit of a fight, and I had to arrest O'Hara. He started giving me a real hard time, but I finally got him in a full Nelson, right from behind, and ran him with his head hard up against a wall, as hard as I could, then let him go, thinking he would fall to the ground, or be dazed or something, but he came charging at me as though nothing had happened, it was as though I had run a bag of cement up against the wall. So he came at me again and I had to take the baton out and melt him. It was the only way to tackle them.

Also tolerated by the police, but for a very different reason to the tolerance shown to the street bookies, was the notorious Raven Club in Renfrew Court at the eastern end of Renfrew Street. The club made no pretensions to comfort or luxury. It consisted simply of several small converted workshops made into a series of interconnecting rooms with a bare minimum of furniture and decoration. It was used for illegal gambling purposes, opened its doors from 11 o'clock at night until the early hours of the morning and became the haunt of some of the hardest criminal elements in Glasgow. The police allowed it to function on the principle that it was better to have all the known criminals in the one place. That way a watch could be kept on them and they could be easily nabbed if necessary, rather than dispersed throughout the district.

The premises were regularly frequented by plain-clothes officers for surveillance purposes, and one of the detectives who knew the club and its variety of visitors well, recounts:

> The Raven was some place, I can tell you. You had some real tough neds from all over the place paying a visit. They went there for a poke from the whores and for card playing and drinking. A wild place it was and I got one or two good arrests there. I remember the McZephyr murder. We called it the McZephyr murder because the guy who was murdered was the guy who played Mr McZephyr on a Coronation Street-type radio programme called the *McFlannels*. The body was found stabbed and strangled in his apartment off the Great Western Road. The trail led to a man called Simpson and we arrested him and he got sent to Peterhead. He escaped, but after a few days we got a wee whisper that he was hanging about in the Raven. So we went in heavy-handed and we got him there, but he didn't put up a fight and gave himself up without any bother.

In the eyes of some, such types are possessed of an aura of glamour and fascination and many otherwise decent and law-abiding citizens frequented the Raven Club in order to rub shoulders with this low-life and to experience the vicarious thrill of associating and gambling with criminals.

For one such thrill seeker a visit to the Raven was to end in tragedy. On the night of 16 August 1960, accompanied by his attractive girlfriend, James Corrigan, a young Glasgow businessman, was finishing off a night on the town with a drink and a flutter on the cards at the Raven. They had enjoyed a night at the Empire and a meal at a city centre restaurant, then, past midnight, had gone on to experience the atmosphere at the club. Good judgment having perhaps been dulled by an excess of alcohol, Corrigan reacted angrily to a remark made to his girlfriend by one of the onlookers. The argument became heated and the two men went into the street to settle their differences. A few moments later Corrigan was found on the pavement outside, dying of several stab wounds inflicted by his assailant.

The detective in charge of the case recalls:

> One night there was a murder at the Raven. A fellow name of Corrigan was there playing cards. He had gone there with his girlfriend after a night out on the town, a real smasher the girl was. They were both decent people who should have known better and should never have gone near the place, but some ordinary people liked to go to places like that and boast about it to their pals afterwards. Anyhow, an argument started with a man called Taylor who was bothering his girl and later outside Taylor stabbed him. Corrigan staggered along the street bleeding and collapsed in front of Henderson's bagpipe shop in Renfrew Street and died on the way to the hospital. Taylor got away in a car and went to a house off the Garscube Road run by a ned called Harry the Horse because he bet a lot on horses and liked to read Damon Runyon. A fellow we knew

called Bailey drove him there. Taylor's trousers were covered in blood so Harry gave him a change of trousers, but they were two sizes too small for him. The next day we got a wee whisper about where he was from one of our touts, so we went up to the house and pinched Taylor. We saw the trousers were too small for him, but even though he had thrown his own trousers away, some of the blood from Taylor's leg had got on the borrowed pair. The blood was from the dead man, so they did just as well for evidence. We went looking for Harry for aiding and abetting and traced him to a house in the Garscube Road. Before we went in we got a wee whisper that he had a gun, so we barged in hard and I grabbed him from the back and my partner big McKinnon started searching him. When big Mac found the gun in a pocket. Harry started to struggle to get away and Big Mac presses the gun in the pocket up against his willie and says to him, 'Struggle and I'll pull the effing trigger.' Harry didn't want shot in the balls so he came quietly after that.

The Raven Club was closed down by the police immediately after that incident.

The Belfast Boat

Saturday night was never a peaceful one in Glasgow and the police did not expect the night of 4 May 1963 to be an exception. Indeed, because of the Rangers—Celtic Scottish Cup Final match due to be played that day at Hampden Park, the police had brought in extra men to deal with the trouble which invariably accompanied a meeting between the two rival Glasgow teams. The game ended in a one–all draw and surprisingly there was no great trouble at the match, with only a score or so arrests for unruly behaviour, no great number for an encounter could sometimes lead to pitched battles in the streets. After the match, the crowds around Hampden dispersed slowly towards home and their favourite pubs, without posing any undue problems for the many police on duty in the neighbouring streets.

There was an exception, however, as one large group of Rangers fans made their way to the Broomielaw to board the steamer that was to take them back home to Belfast. This steamer, known as 'The Belfast Boat', provided a regular daily service between Glasgow and Belfast, transporting goods and passengers. The steamer had another traditional function. On the days when the Orange Order held their marches in either one of the cities, it carried ardent Orangemen between the two places, and on the occasion of Rangers—Celtic matches the boat was taken over by Rangers supporters coming from Belfast to support their team.

On these occasions the supporters of 'the green' eschewed the use of that particular means of transport for two reasons; the mixture would have been far too explosive, and the greens, always outnumbered by at least three to one, would have been swamped by the opposition in the fracas that would have ensued. The bulk of the supporters who travelled for the football matches looked upon the trip to Glasgow as an opportunity to get roaring drunk and let off steam in the charged atmosphere of the Old Firm football match. Of course, decent and properly behaved people also made the trip on these occasions, but they invariably travelled below decks in cabin class, with their own bar and lounge area, well isolated from the rabble above.

This particular group from Belfast were even rougher than the usual supporter at the Rangers' games and had drunk their way steadily from Hampden to the Broomielaw, singing and bawling partisan songs and leaving behind them a trail of broken beer glasses, bloody noses and smashed shop windows. They arrived at the ship determined to have one more drink at a pub facing the gangplank before going on board. The pub, 'Betty's Bar' was owned by Peter Keenan, the Scottish boxing champion, and staffed by two of his sparring partners. The two barmen were in the process of closing the premises when the mob descended on them, demanding entry. The request was refused, whereupon the two barmen were pulled away from the door and thrown into the street by the mob, who then proceeded to wreck the pub and help themselves to all the drink they could carry on to the steamer. The policeman on the beat was passing by at the time, took one look at the milling mob and promptly went to the nearest police box to call for assistance.

The following is the official account of what happened next, as written in the chief constable's report for the year 1963:

Police Escort On Vessel To Belfast

On 4th May 1963, a football match was played in Glasgow between the Rangers and Celtic clubs. Several hundred supporters of the teams had journeyed from Belfast and were returning aboard a motor vessel, which sailed from Lancefield Quay at 9pm carrying 1,076 passengers. The vessel had travelled a few hundred yards down the river when a number of the passengers became disorderly and a member of the crew was assaulted.

The vessel returned to the quayside and the police were informed. Police officers were drawn from all divisions and on their appearance the disorder among the passengers died away. Four passengers were arrested for disorder. Several of the crew were unwilling to sail without police escort, and I held a discussion with representatives of the company operating the ship. It was agreed to send one inspector, two sergeants and 24 constables on the vessel at the expense of the shipping company. All the men who went were volunteers.

During the voyage the police patrolled the vessel and there was no further trouble. The Glasgow police party was flown back from Belfast the following day at the expense of the shipping company.

That is the somewhat bland official report of the matter. Here follows the reality of the incident as told by one of the constables involved:

The Belfast boats used to dock at the Broomielaw. One Saturday after a Celtic—Rangers match the mob came down to the Broomielaw to get on the boat. They were all roaring drunk and had been rampaging all the way along from Hampden. Peter Keenan the boxer used to have a pub there, Betty's Bar it was called. It was ready to close when these guys come in demanding drink. When they got refused they just smashed the bar up and started helping themselves. The man on the beat couldn't do anything alone, so some other cops arrived. By this time the neds had taken all the drink they could carry on to the boat, but that wasn't enough for them. The boat had just sailed when they broke into the bar on board ship for more drink and then went down and started breaking into the cabins where decent people were and terrorising them. A seaman was nearly killed trying to stop them, he lost an eye in the fight. The skipper turned back and refused to leave with that mob and called headquarters. The night shifts were just coming on and men from every division were called in. Our inspector, Alan Mitchell, says to us 'there's a riot at Broomielaw'.

There was me, and Big John, and Big McGarvey, about eight or nine of us, all hand-picked men from our division, and about 70 from all over. When we got there it was a bloody shambles. Neds running about crazy drunk and throwing empty bottles from the ship down at us. They had thrown a wounded seaman down the gangplank and he was in a helluva mess, face all covered in blood. The chief constable had come down to see for himself, it was that bad. The bottles were raining down from the ship on to the polis on the quay below. The place was covered in broken glass and there were yells and shouts for help coming from some of the passengers with their heads stuck out of the portholes. The chief looks at the shambles for a while then consults with some of his big brass there from headquarters then says to us:

'I don't care how, but stop it.'

Once we heard that we knew what we had to do.

We fought our way up the gangplank, the usual narrow thing, it could have been easily defended, but we hammered up to the top hitting as hard as we could. They were all mad drunk. It's not hard to beat a drunk man as long as he doesn't get a grip on you. They can't move as fast as a sober man can, so you just stay at arm's length and belt them. There was this one guy stripped to the waist, he was throwing bottles at us from the deck. We charged and that man vanished under an avalanche of polis. When I got to the top, I remember one bloke, he comes charging down with a fire-axe in his hands, Big John ducks under it and breaks his knees with the baton and that guy gets swamped by polis too. After a while we got the deck cleared and all the trouble-makers locked up in the deck lounge.

By this time all the fight's been knocked out of them and they're all sitting around holding their sore heads. But the skipper says, 'there's trouble downstairs,' so we went down below decks, right enough, there were more neds going mad down there, smashing into cabins and assaulting passengers. Right, out with the batons again. We charged, we got right into them, that was some fight. We really got into them and knocked a dozen of them stiff and that was the fight out of them too. The chief constable didn't want any of them in our cells, so we had orders to keep the neds on the boat, to pacify them and send them back to Belfast and let the police there make charges. But when the fighting was over the captain refused to sail without a police escort. The chief asked for volunteers and about 30 of us went. So we went to Belfast with the boat but we had no more trouble, those neds had had enough.

The passengers wouldn't come out of their cabins, though, They were all scared out of their lives and had barricaded themselves in. I don't blame them, I'd never seen anyone as mad with drink as that lot. I'd been everywhere in the world except Ireland. I always wanted to get to Ireland to see the place, that's why I volunteered to go, but I only took about 12 steps there, from the boat to a van to the airport. Got flown back right away and didn't see a thing there. When the neds came off the boat at Belfast they were in quite some state, bashed up, heads split, bleeding all over the place, in some mess. Robertson was chief constable then. When the Irish police chief sees the state the neds are in he says:

'I hope nobody thinks my men did that, my men wouldn't do that, that was Robertson's rascals did that.'

The name stuck and from then on we were called Robertson's rascals. We didn't get anything extra for that, we were just coming on night shift and that was part of our job. I don't know if anybody got paid any extra, I don't think so, there was no overtime in those days. There were no complaints against us either. If the neds got tough they knew what to expect and they couldn't get any tougher than they were on that boat.

Rangers won the replay match on the following Wednesday by three goals to one.

Betty Alexander

The Garnethill area of the Cowcaddens begins at the east of Renfrew Street. In the fifties Garnethill was almost exclusively made up of large dwelling houses and superior quality tenements, dominated architecturally by St Aloysius church in Rose Street and Charles Rennie Mackintosh's School of Art building in Renfrew Street a few yards away. The area had few shops of any consequence and so the inhabitants had to do most of their shopping in the Cambridge Street area, which to all intents and purposes was part of the Cowcaddens district. The large houses of Garnethill, built at the end of the nineteenth century for the use of the rich merchants of the city, were now almost all used as small bed and breakfast hotels and lodging houses, much sought after by travelling salesmen and by the scores of music hall artistes who appeared weekly at the city centre theatres. The tenements were inhabited by 'respectable', working class families who considered themselves a cut above the inhabitants of the tenements in the Cowcaddens proper.

One such was the Alexander family who lived in a neat and well tended flat in a tenement at 43 Buccleuch Street, in the shadow of St Aloysius, their parish church. The jewel of the Alexander household was their little daughter Betty, a friendly, vivacious and pretty four-year-old girl. The child was well known to everyone in the district as she played with her friends in the street and accompanied her mother on shopping trips to the local shops, or going for the messages. As a special Saturday treat from her fourth birthday onwards, a visit to the pictures was always laid on by the parents, which consisted of a matinee visit to one of the many cinemas in the area which would be showing some film or cartoon suitable for children. There was hardly a cinema usherette or shop assistant who did not know wee Betty Alexander.

The little girl was not due to start school until the age of five but she attended a nursery in New City Road, about five minutes walk away from her home. Her parents took her there on four mornings each week and she was collected either by them or by one of the neighbours at midday, at which time, after midday 'piece', she would go off to play happily with other children of the district. In the absence of parks and supervised centres, tenement backyards and street pavements served the children as a playground.

There was little crime in the district. Each little tenement community was very close-knit and anyone with anti-social tendencies would immediately be disciplined by parents or neighbours, and, most important of all, by the 'polis' on the beat, who, often at the request of the parents, would administer a summary cuffing to any youth found in transgression of the law. The man on the beat knew the name of every family in his area, and in law-abiding districts such as Garnethill he was friendly with mostly everyone. He was part of the community, known to everyone by his first name, the first one to call on when any problem arose and the first one to turn to for advice. In view of all these relationships, parents thought it perfectly safe, after a few routine admonitions, to allow their children to play in the streets and backyards unsupervised.

Child molestation certainly must have existed – it seems hardly likely that such activity could be just a modern phenomenon, but if it did, little, if any, publicity was given to it in the media. The Alexanders thought nothing of allowing little Betty to roam around alone in the streets and backyards to play with her friends as her shouted name would always suffice to bring her home when required. No one thought of the Garnethill area as being unsafe for children until the night that little Betty disappeared.

It was the night of 7 October 1952. The weather had been good in Glasgow that summer, the warm, sunny days had carried over into the beginning of autumn and the children were allowed to play outside well into the onset of dusk. Betty's mother had prepared the evening meal and went into the close to call in her daughter, whom she had seen playing in the backyard some minutes before. She shouted several times, but no Betty appeared. As the minutes ticked by with no response to her cries a cold and gnawing worry began to take hold and she set off in search of her daughter, shouting her name at the top of her voice. She banged on the doors of neighbouring houses. All the other children were already inside, but there was no sign of her little Betty, and no one had seen her during the last half-hour.

The police were hurriedly called and an immediate search of all the backyards and closes in the area was started. Darkness had by now set in and beams of light from police torches criss-crossed the night as they hurried from close to close and backyard to backyard, incessantly shouting the girl's name, hoping against hope for an answer. No trace of the little girl could be found. The search carried on through the night. Neighbours joined in the search, every backyard, every midden, every possible hiding place was searched, but to no avail. Little Betty Alexander had simply vanished from the face of the earth.

Next morning the biggest search ever mounted by the Glasgow police began. The head of the Northern Division CID, Neil Beaton, put every available man on the streets to search for the little girl. Detective Superintendent Robert Calhoun brought in extra men from outlying divisions to assist and literally hundreds of neighbours joined in the search. Someone reported having seen the little girl in the company of a man in Trerons department store in Sauchiehall Street on the day of her disappearance. The street was cordoned off and the store closed and searched from top to bottom by scores of police and firemen, but to no avail. Finally, on 9 October, two days after her disappearance, the dead body of the missing girl was discovered hidden in a backyard in Buccleuch Lane.

Within minutes of the discovery of the body the whole area was sealed off. Squads of detectives, photographers, fingerprint experts, specially trained men from the CID and scores of uniformed police began combing the area for clues. Never before had so much manpower been focused on the solution of a crime and such an intense manhunt would not be seen again for more than 20 years, until the search for Bible John was to begin.

At the height of the investigation more than 200 detectives participated, many of them brought in from other divisions. The postmortem examination of the little girl had revealed that she had eaten a meal shortly before her death and that the food consumed was not of the same kind taken at her last meal at home. This suggested that she had not been murdered immediately after her abduction, but had been kept prisoner in some household and fed there. Two thousand houses in the area were searched by squads of police and the food in them examined. Every shop, every workplace and every household within a quarter mile radius of Betty's home was visited and the occupants closely questioned. Every male in Garnethill over the age of 17, a total of 1,500, was finger-printed in an attempt to match some smudged prints found near the body. Statements were taken from thousands of people and, in all, 3,000 reports were closely examined in the Maitland Street station. An exhaustive check on the movement of every man, woman and child to be found in the district was made. Pedestrians were stopped in the street and questioned on their movements and the reason for their presence in the district, but no one could give the police the slightest indication as to who the murderer of wee Betty might be. After three days of enquiries few facts had emerged. A long time was required to go through the fingerprints of 1,500 men, the computer had as yet not been invented, and meticulously slow comparisons had to be made by hand. All statements had to be checked for any discrepancy that might turn out to be a vital clue. Near the scene of the discovery of the body half a fingerprint had been found, and it was the matching of this fragment that gave the police some hope. It was never divulged where the fingerprint had come from, although it was known that a sheet of paper had been found next to the body and this may have been the source.

When the body was found, the condition of the child's clothes seemed to indicate that Betty had been killed elsewhere and the body taken to the yard where it was found. Her dress was dry, yet it had rained quite heavily in the area 24 hours after she had vanished. Moreover, the yard had been searched by neighbours at the time of the disappearance and nothing had been discovered there.

Everything about the crime suggested that the murder had been committed by someone who knew the district well. The house adjacent to the yard had been empty for some time, and the yard itself was in a very secluded spot. The body had been placed on some steps at the inside of the entrance, which was heavily padlocked. The only other entrance was a narrow passageway from West Graham Street that was not visible from the road and it was highly unlikely that a stranger to the district could have known of its existence.

Finally, three people, two men and a woman, were taken to the station for questioning, They were kept there overnight, but were released without any comment on the part of the police.

All sorts of rumours circulated; crowds in their hundreds gathered at Maitland Street police station to await news; every coming and going from the station was observed and commented upon. Rumour fed on rumour. Crowds stood for hours in front of Trerons even after the search had ceased. The place had been searched, therefore something must have gone on there, it was reasoned. It was rumoured that the police were on the lookout for a plain brown van seen in the street at the time of Betty's disappearance. Vigilante groups took to stopping and searching vans of that description and had to be dispersed by the police. The minister of the Episcopalian Church in Garnethill formed groups of parents for a 'child patrol', whose duty it would be to watch over every activity of the children of the area and to escort them to and from school. The dreadful crime had given birth to something akin to mass hysteria in the neighbourhood.

Suspicion for the crime centred on the caretaker of a local dispensary, Old Tom, who lived alone; a stone's throw from the yard where the body was found. He was a recluse who did his job and seldom spoke to anybody, and was the butt of jokes of the local children. There was something in his demeanour and his evasive answers to questions that aroused police suspicion, and he was taken back and forth to the Maitland Street police station over the course of some days and subjected to relentless questioning in an attempt to break down his constant protestations of innocence. He was stripped and searched and his body and clothing meticulously examined. His home was gone over with a fine toothcomb and everything in it subjected to a meticulous examination. The meagre contents of his kitchen and the scraps of food in it were carefully looked at. There was no evidence that Betty had ever been to the house or that the food found in her stomach had originated in that kitchen. Forensic science was in its infancy in those days and where nowadays a DNA test might have resolved everything, there was no evidence to justify the arrest of the old man on a charge of murder.

Taking part in the investigation was a young policeman, Joe Beattie, just elevated to the ranks of the CID. During the war he had seen service with the RAF as a bomber pilot, had joined the force in 1946 after being demobbed with an outstanding war record. This was his first murder case. In his retirement, after a brilliant career during which he received more than 30 commendations, Joe Beattie would often muse on the irony of the fact that the first murder case he was involved in had remained unsolved, as had his last case some 25 years later. His last case was the Bible John murders, where, as detective superintendent, Joe was in charge of the later stages of the investigation.

Despite months of unrelenting effort, the murder of Betty Alexander was never solved. Her death cast a dark shadow of fear on Garnethill and Cowcaddens and, for a time afterwards, little groups of vigilantes stood by as their children played on the pavements and in the backyards of the area. The caretaker's comings and goings at the station had been well noted. Everyone believed him guilty and after the interrogations he never returned to his home for fear of retribution. He was rumoured to have died in a model lodging house at Anderston Cross some months later.

Informers

To a very large extent the solving of a crime and bringing the guilty parties to justice depended on the services of informers. Each beat policeman and each CID detective cultivated his own tout and had his own method of doing so. This was usually done by gaining the confidence and trust of some petty criminal by conceding him a small favour and then suggesting that a quid pro quo in the shape of information would be appreciated. These favours sometimes took the form of letting an offender know that one or other of his shady activities were known to the policeman in question, but that they would be overlooked. Sometimes the favour consisted of helping the prisoner's family in some way when the so-called breadwinner was in prison. There was no Department of Social Security then. The local authority usually ran its own help schemes for the poor as best as it could: these services became known as 'The Parish', and a favourable word from someone in authority such as a policeman was always useful in an approach to the local council for help.

Occasionally the informer would simply give information for money and a special fund was kept for these payments. The fund could be accessed only by members of the CID; a beat man had to make his own arrangements with the tout. Sometimes the informer would be of a type who basked in the feigned admiration of 'his' policeman and would go out of his way to obtain their approval by supplying information on the latest crime committed in the district. This could be done in a variety of ways. A watchful eye could be kept on the spending habits of other criminals after a robbery or safe-breaking had taken place. So-and-so would be lavish in standing drinks for his friends after a local house-breaking incident. So-and-so would bet an inordinate amount on the horses or at the dog tracks. These activities would be noted and passed on to the mentor. Once a bond of trust had been established, a tout would usually work for only his 'own' policeman and trust no other with information, and the policeman would never divulge the identity of his tout or touts to anyone, not even to his colleagues.

Great care had to be exercised in the use of these informers, and their identity kept secret, for should the hard criminals in the district ever become suspicious that one of their kind had turned tout, the consequences for them would have been disastrous. Many were the fatal beatings adminis-tered to those suspected of being informers, so a streetwise policeman would be very even-handed in his approach to the neds on his beat. No extra leniency would be shown to his informers during raids on toss pitches, bookie's premises or shebeens. They would be given exactly the same rough treatment as anyone else caught in breach of the law, and no more time would be spent talking to them in the open than would be granted to any other criminal in the district.

One policeman recalls:

> I had a great tout who gave me dozens of arrests. His name was Dots ———. He had 79 convictions against him for breach of the peace, malicious damage and drunk and disorderly, but more than half of them were done to give us information. He'd deliberately get himself arrested so's he could give us a whisper. He lived in digs up the Garscube Road, and hung around half a dozen pubs and shebeens there when he had money, and kept his eyes and ears open. When he had no money or when he was too drunk

his landlady used to throw him out. He would get a bed in the model in McPhater Street next to the station for the night, and sometimes they had to call us in when he started a fight with one of the other lodgers there. So we would run him in for a breach of the peace and when he was locked up in the cells he'd give us a whisper about this or that he had picked up in the pubs and we would give him a couple of bob from a fund we kept for the touts. But only the CID could tap the fund, the beat man had to make his own arrangement with Dots.

You had to have money up front to get a bed in the model, a shilling it was, paid in advance, and sometimes when he was broke and his landlady had tossed him out he'd come out to Maitland Street and start a row outside the station, cursing and swearing and effing and ceeing and yelling at passers-by and creating a general disturbance. He used to take a boot off and throw it through the window of the station and we used to run him in for malicious damage and put him in a cell for the night. Dozens of times he did it. Sometimes he did it because he had information and wanted to get inside to give it to us, but sometimes he did it simply to get a warm kip for the night and a mug of tea and a piece with margarine in the morning. He was about 30 years of age but he was in terrible condition and looked 60. Never ate properly and drank cheap booze all day long and meths with it.

Well, one morning at seven o'clock my mate and I are coming in from the night shift and we see something lying next to the steps at the station door. We take a close look and we saw it was a body. It was Dots and he was dead, as stiff as a doornail he was and it looked as though he had been lying there all night. So we call the van to get him taken away to the hospital for certification. Any body you found, and there were plenty of them around in the winter, had to be sent to a hospital for certification, no matter how dead they were. Just as Dots' body's getting loaded into the van we notice that he's only got one boot on. So we look around a bit, and there's his other boot lying up against the wall under a window. He must have thrown it to smash the glass but missed the window and he dropped down and didn't have the strength to crawl up the station steps and died. It's a shame when you think of it. Maybe if his aim had been better and he'd smashed the window he would have been taken inside and maybe he wouldn't have died. That was a shame. We lost a first class source there. Many was the good whisper he gave us.

One night in the late fifties, a daring and puzzling robbery took place in Forsyth's, an up-market gent's clothier at the corner of Renfield Street and Gordon Street. A safe in the manager's office had been blown and a sum in excess of £4,000 had been taken. There was no sign of a forced entry into the office, which was on the third floor of the building, nor was there the slightest clue as to how the thief had got away with his loot. Every member of the staff was questioned closely, but no clue emerged as to how or who could have done the robbery. Every tout in the Northern was put on alert but not a whisper was forthcoming as to possible perpetrators, and after all sources of information had been exhausted the affair was put away amongst the unsolved crimes file.

One day, about six months later, a whisper came down from a prostitute who worked a lucrative city centre beat. Prostitutes were easily recruited into the ranks of informers. Their trade brought them into regular contact with the underworld and into regular conflict with the police. The occasional show of leniency in return for any information they might be able provide often brought rich rewards. This particular prostitute had already been approached by a detective to whom she owed a debt of gratitude and she had been asked by him to be on the alert for any crumb of information she might be able to glean about the Forsyth robbery. Vera, as she was known, worked a pitch in Buchanan Street close by a Presbyterian church. Her debt to the detective was of long standing and stemmed from something that had happened to her there some years before. A large and imposing sign which read: 'Have you sinned today?' had been erected outside this place of worship, and one day the enterprising Vera wrote underneath in lipstick: 'If not, phone this number' followed by her home phone number. One of the beat men, a member of the Plymouth brethren, saw no humour at all in this, and proceeded to give Vera a very hard time, harassing her at every opportunity and made her life a misery. He was eventually told to ease up by his superior, who had been given one or two good whispers in the past by Vera, and who, if truth be told, was rather amused by the incident. Vera's gratitude knew no bounds and her efforts on her mentor's behalf doubled.

Her whisper to him was that a certain Sammy Davidson who lived in Port Dundas might profitably be questioned about the safe-blowing. The investigating detective takes up the story:

> So I go up to see Sammy. I found him in the Dog House where he always drank, Jackson's big fancy place in Dundas Street. Funny name that for a pub, I never found out who had got the idea for a name like that. Anyhow, Sammy was a sharp wee ned, not violent but very cunning. So I go up to the bar and

stand him a drink and start to butter him up a wee bit and say, 'I hear from a whisper it was you who did Forsyth's,' and he says, 'Naw, who telt you that?' and I say, 'It musta been you, nobody else that I know had the brains to do it,' and he looks a wee bit proud and says, 'Naw it wisnae me,' and I say, 'Come on, how did you get in? You've got us all with our bums out the window up there at headquarters, we huvnae a clue how it was done, it musta taken a good bit of nerve too, and anyhow, even if it was you we huvnae any proof, but I'd just like to know, it was such a good job.' Sammy blows his nose and scratches his head and taps the side of his nose and puts on a wise look and says, 'Naw, it wisnae me, but I know how it was done,' and I say, 'Come on tell me, I canny do anything about it without proof. We've got no fingerprints or the loot or anything, so it disnae matter if you tell me. I'd just like to know, it must have been done real smart to get in and out, go on, how was it done?' So he footers about a bit and I stand him another drink and butter him up a bit more and finally he tells me: 'Ah'm no sayin' it was me, mind you, but if it was, I woulda climbed up the back rone in Cranston's Lane [a full block away from Forsyth's] right up to the roof. Then right along the roof to the top of Forsyth's. There are some flagpoles there, and I would have shinned down one of the ropes to the office window, then jemmied it open with no damage, got in, did the job, put the loot in a rucksack and back out again, shut the window, up the rope, back over the roof, leave no trace and down the rone, and away.'

'Gee, that was really smart,' I say. 'I wouldnae have believed it. You know Sammy, I think it was you did it.

I could put two men on you 24 hours a day for long enough and find the loot, and you'd get done, two years at least, but it would take too much time and it's no worth the bother. So I'll tell you what, if you give me a wee whisper now and then about anything you hear I'll forget you ever spoke to me.'

He wasn't to know that there was no way at all I could ever have got the manpower to do as I had threatened. So he became one of my best touts and I made a lot of good cops from his information. One time later on he got done for stealing metals from a place up on the canal banks, copper and lead and stuff like that, and he was sent to Barlinnie for six months. He even sent me information from there, in the form of a coded letter. While he was in there I helped his family and told him I'd found him a job if he went straight, and he was grateful and sent me this letter from Barlinnie:

Dear Joe,

just a few lines to let you know that my wife was up last night, & she told me about you going to see Mr Bruce about a job for me, it is a chance in a 1000 and I'll snatch at it, as long as he is willing to wait untill I get out on the 21st Dec. Will he wait that long Joe? Anyway, thanks, & thanks also for seeing the factor for me. I'll sqaure you up as soon as I see you, as a house in Possil will be a big improvement on where I'm staying just now. I got the offer of one in Grove Street, above the Albert Bar, but the wife didn't fancy that mate of mine that runs around there, you know, Harry, a quiet soul, who will not say boo to a sheep, but Margaret just can't take to him.

Well, Joe, I'll bet ...

In it he's telling me who had done a certain job and

where the loot is. He was a smart wee man, and he did take that job and he did go straight but about two years later he was found murdered one night up a close in Lyon Street. Never found out why or who done it. Mark you, you could have been murdered for a Woodbine up Lyon Street. So we lost a good tout there. I remember the very last whisper he gave me. One time in the New Savoy, the picture house at the corner of Hope Street and Renfrew Street, there was a Western film running. *The Great Train Robbery*, a remake of the first Western ever made. I forget the name of the star. The cinema foyer had been turned into a Wild West arena and it was a real great show and fairly drew the crowds. A model train all decked up as an old puffer with a high smokestack, real Western style, ran in and out of mountains and canyons, real Western country. It was a lovely model, beautifully made and very artistic, about three feet long and more, a super Hornby train type thing. Well, one day somebody stole the train, believe it or not. Talk about the Great Train Robbery! Two guys came into the foyer, said the train had to be repaired, lifted it up and loaded it into a van and off. How they ever hoped to get rid of it and get money for it God only knows. But some neds would steal anything that wasn't nailed down just for the sake of it. Anyhow, I got a whisper from Sammy that two brothers had nicked it, so two of us went up to Swan Street where they lived. But they had moved to Blackhill. So we went up to Blackhill, though we didn't fancy going up there, it was a bloody awful place and you had to watch your back. When we went into the close we could feel a blast of heat coming out. It was the middle of winter and we could feel the hot air coming out of the close mouth. So we went into the ground floor flat where they were and there, in a corner, was the train. The heat in the house was terrible. They had all the electric fires turned on, even the electric oven and cooker were on. They had the hot water running, everything. They had tapped the main cable and couldn't turn the electricity off, so the place was roasting with free heat. They got done for the two things, for the train and for the electricity. Fess Parker the actor's name was, I remember now. That was the last whisper I ever got from Sammy. I don't think he was done for being a tout. I would have got to know.

One day I got a whisper from a shopkeeper in the Queen's Arcade. This bloke was the last man I would ever have thought I'd get a whisper from, because he was a resetter we'd had our eye on for a long time and was a real shifty character. He would order a lorry load of goods stolen from a factory in the Midlands and get it driven up and dispose of it to various places here. If you do anything like that you have to have the money ready up front to pay for it when it arrives and if you don't you're in big trouble with the neds who've done the job, because how are they going to get rid of the loot if it's an on order job?

One day he's ordered up a load of stuff, but just before it's due to arrive, he loses all his money on the dogs and he's got no money to pay for it. So rather than face the neds with no money to pay them he gives me the whisper about the lorry coming up with stolen goods and we nab it and the two drivers. They couldn't figure out how we knew about them. Christ knows what they would have done to him when they came out of jail six months later if they had known who had snitched on them.

There were also many ordinary citizens who kept their eyes open in the course of their daily work, noted any unusual activity and who could give invaluable information to the man on the beat. One of the constables on the busy Hope Street beat recalls:

> We had a real great system going for us there with people who kept their eyes open on the street. Don't forget, there was Paterson's Garage in Hope Street with 60 drivers. That was 60 pairs of eyes we had working for us, they didn't want any neds around and they wanted to keep in with us, so if they saw anything suspicious they would give us a whisper. We knew every one of them by name. There were four newsvendors in Sauchie in the space of one block. They were easy meat for anyone at the demand, so we took care of them, and they would keep their eyes open and when we passed they would give us a wee nod if everything was OK. If they had anything to tell us they would pretend to go for a piss to the Savoy or a pub or some other place and we'd go there to get the whisper. We didn't want to be seen talking to them out in the open because any neds hanging around would suspect. Then there were the nightwatchmen, security guards they call them now. They would keep their eyes open too and give us the nod if anything suspicious was going on. We didn't spend too much time talking to them because, again, if there were any neds watching they didn't want them to think they were too friendly with the polis. These guys were very exposed at night. They usually sat in a wee, open hut with a

brazier to keep them warm and could very easily get done by the neds.

We had one fella who was absolutely fantastic and gave us dozens of arrests. He was the night-watchman for Boots in Sauchiehall Street opposite the Gaumont picture house. He had a wee office on the very top floor with a sort of bay window, and he could see up and down the length of Sauchiehall Street. The things he could see from there during the night! He had a phone in the place and if he saw anything suspicious he phoned the office right away to let them know. The office would set the light on the boxes flashing to get us to phone in and give us his information. Many's the good arrest we got that way. The neds wondered how the hell they had been found out. Talk about your modern closed circuit TV cameras!

Bad Eggs

Stringent physical tests were applied to recruits on enlistment. By 1950 the minimum height requirement was five feet ten inches, and the applicant's medical history was gone into thoroughly. Background and character were also investigated before the recruit was accepted for training and during the two-year probationary period close watch would be kept on the rookie's general behaviour. Character is an impossible quality to evaluate over a short period of time and occasionally, in spite of the screening process, the occasional egg which turned out bad was accepted into the force.

In 1950, James Robertson, 35, an experienced constable who was married with two young children, had been assigned to work a beat in the Gorbals. It was far from being an inspiring area to patrol, to say the least. It consisted mainly of row after row of grimy, squalid tenements with rat-infested backyards, some shops and a variety of small workshops, all too small to warrant the use of a night-watchman. These tenements were terrible places to live in. Including the pavement level flat, there were four floors with three houses on each floor and one lavatory to serve the 12 houses. They formed the background for a catalogue of squalid crimes by the local hooligans ranging from frequent razor slashings and domestic violence to thefts from shops and houses. Night shifts were particularly depressing and stressful for an officer assigned to such an area. There were no cinemas or workplaces available where a warm cup of tea, a blether and perhaps a game of cards could be shared with the nightwatchman on duty after the obligatory rounds of the beat had been made.

One particularly wet and windy night near midnight, shortly after the beginning of his shift, Robertson's attention was taken by the sudden appearance of a woman, who had come out from a close behind him and was running to overtake him. The tenement houses of the poorer districts were equipped with penny-in-the-slot gas meters which had to be supplied regularly with coins to keep the gas flowing and the lady had run out of coppers and was looking for change of a threepenny bit to feed the meter. Catherine McCluskey had seen the policeman pass in front of her ground floor window and had hoped he might have some change in his pocket. He had, and after a few words of conversation the constable was invited in from the wind and rain to partake of a warm cuppa. Much more than a cup of tea was partaken of, and now, a warm refuge from the cold and rainy streets having been found, frequent night visits to the house were made and the same pleasures indulged in by Constable Robertson. After some weeks Catherine suggested that her favours should be recognised by the appearance of some money, and Robertson, who had a wife and two children to keep on a policeman's wage of ten pounds a week could not find his way to do so. A heated argument followed during which Robertson lost his temper and hit Catherine a backhanded blow across the face. She fell heavily, striking her head against the iron fender in front of the gas fire and lay as if dead.

After all this drama Robertson finished the patrolling of his shift as though nothing had happened, reporting to his headquarters from the boxes on the beat and filling in the journals there as duty required. All of this time he had been formulating a plan of action, and later in the night he broke into a van parked in a side street and drove it to the house where the body of his erstwhile lady love lay in a pool of blood. He wrapped the woman in a sheet, carried the bundle out into the van and drove with it to Prospecthill Road, a distance of nearly two miles from the scene of the crime. He removed the sheet, laid her body cross-wise on the road and then proceeded to run over it with the vehicle to make the scene appear to be the result of a hit-and-run accident. But then, in an act of irrationality, which proved to be his downfall, before driving away he reversed the vehicle over the corpse, presumably to make absolutely sure that Catherine was dead.

He then drove back to his beat in the Gorbals, the van was replaced on the spot he had stolen it from and he continued on his duties as if nothing had happened until relieved at seven o'clock in the morning. At about the same time as he was finishing his shift, a passing lorry driver in Prospecthill Road saw the body lying in the middle of the road and immediately called the police. The first impression was the one Robertson had intended to convey, that the poor woman had been the victim of a hit and run driver, and this was the immediate conclusion of the detective inspector who first arrived on the scene. Then Constable Kevin, the driver of a patrol car that had been called to the accident, remarked on something that had gone unnoticed by his senior colleagues. He brought to their attention that the tyre marks on the greasy road and the marks on the body were a clear indication that the vehicle involved had reversed over the body before driving away. Why should a hit-and-run driver do such a thing?

Then another fact was noticed and another question asked. With the body in such a mangled condition, where was all the blood that should have been present on the road at the scene of such an occurrence? There was little or no blood on the road, yet the injuries sustained by the woman should have caused her body to bleed extensively. Could it be that the woman had been killed somewhere else and the body placed as it was to simulate a road accident? The investigation started with the identification of the dead woman and an examination of her home showed clearly where she had died, or at best been seriously wounded. A squad of detectives immediately started to work on the case and everyone in the surrounding area was interrogated, including Robertson himself, who, after all had been the man on the beat at the time of the woman's death. He claimed to have seen nothing unusual during his shift and suspicion did not immediately fall on him, but then a young man who lived two closes away supplied the police with a vital piece of information. This man often met his girlfriend on the first floor landing of the close where the murdered woman lived. To escape prying eyes, he would turn off the gas light on the landing, and sometimes he would see a uniformed policeman tapping on the back window and being admitted into the house of the murdered woman.

Immediately the investigation focused on Robertson and soon it became obvious that the policeman was the guilty man.

He was arrested and tried for murder at the High Court. On every day of the trial there were queues of people hoping to gain entry to hear the sordid details of the case. Robertson was represented by the famous defence lawyer, Mr Lawrence Dowdall, but as the evidence against him was presented, it became obvious that there could only be one verdict. The evidence of the courting couple on the landing, the finding of blood specks on his uniform which matched the blood type of his victim, his fingerprints found in the woman's house, traces of the victim's blood left in the van used for taking it to Prospecthill Road, tyres on the van which matched the tyre tracks found on the road by the dead body, all pointed to the guilt of Robertson. He sat with his head bowed during the long trial, never once looking at his wife who sat expressionless through each moment of the proceedings.

After a short deliberation, the jury returned a verdict of guilty and he was duly hanged at Barlinnie prison in December 1950. No one claimed Robertson's body and he was buried in the little graveyard inside the walls of the prison.

By his action Robertson had forfeited all his police pension rights and his widow and two children were left penniless. His colleagues started a collection for her and began to canvass shops and business premises in the Glasgow area for donations. The collection met with a generous response, the gifts ranging from ten shillings from lowly members of staff to a handsome cheque for £1500 from the owner of one of the large department stores in Sauchiehall Street. With the money thus collected, the widow emigrated to Canada with her children, there to begin a new life.

Some years later another and much more spectacular case involving perpetrators with police backgrounds gripped the attention of the city.

Howard Wilson was a bright and enthusiastic young man with the prospects of a promising career ahead of him when he joined the police in December 1958. The son of a south side newsagent, he had a good education at Glasgow Academy and with this background and the ambition that went with it, he looked forward to the prospect of quick advancement. However, career advancement in the police, unless the individual is possessed of very exceptional qualities, is usually a slow and methodical process. Prime emphasis is put on the acquisition of knowledge and experience before promotion is given in the force, and Wilson did not have the patience required to acquire these necessary qualities.

He served for a time as turnkey at the Central Division, a position with advancement potential, but he was soon back on the beat as an ordinary constable and despite three commenda-tions by the chief constable, the prospects for promotion seemed as far way as ever. In 1967, after serving for nine years, in his late twenties and with a wife and two children to support, he decided to resign from the force to seek financial betterment and opened a greengrocers shop in Allison Street in the vicinity of the Craigie Street police station.

During his period of service he had become a member of a local shooting club, where he practised regularly with two ex-policemen friends. John Sim and Ian Donaldson, had resigned at about the same time as Wilson, also to set up their own businesses. The three kept up their membership at the club, where they met on a regular basis, there to discuss the problems encountered in common in the pursuit of financial success. Things had gone badly for the three of them. To make money in business had not turned out to be as easy as they had imagined, the pitfalls were many and they each faced the prospect of financial ruin in their respective enterprises.

Because of the expertise acquired as police, the three imagined they knew the way to commit a crime which would solve their financial troubles and to this end they planned what was to have been the perfect robbery, a bank hold-up. The bank chosen for their raid was the British Linen Bank in Giffnock, and for weeks they studied the premises and formulated a plan of action. On 16 July 1969, brandishing handguns and with their faces masked, the three charged into the bank, tied up the staff, and forced one of them to open the safe. All the cash in the safe was put into canvas bags and the three took off in a waiting car with the £20,000 proceeds of the robbery. The car was driven by a young man, Joe McGeachy, a business partner of Wilson, who had been persuaded by him to join the gang for that purpose. The raid was cleanly and expertly carried out, the robbers had left no clues to their identity, and after a fruitless investigation the police put the case into their unsolved files.

The money did not last long. The stolen cash eased the

78

immediate pressures on the three, but business continued to go badly for them, debts once more began to build up and six months later Wilson decided to embark on another similar venture, this time at the Clydesdale Bank in Linwood. Two of his companions, Donaldson and Sim agreed, but McGeachy could not be persuaded and refused to join in with them. McGeachy was never seen again, and in later years, the whisper, impossible to corroborate of course, was that he had been done away with and his body disposed of in one of the cement pillars of the Kingston bridge which was under construction at the time. It was rumoured that Wilson had paid a criminal known to him from his days in the force to get rid of McGeachy in this manner.

The raid on the Linwood bank took place just after Christmas 1969 and more or less followed the same procedure as the first robbery. The staff were threatened with pistols, a knife was placed at the manager's throat and, under threat of death, he was made to open the safe door. The thieves had brought three suitcases into the bank with them. These they proceeded to fill with the banknotes stacked inside the safe, and again the getaway was made in a car left parked outside. In the absence of McGeachy, one of the trio drove the vehicle.

Wilson lived in a ground floor flat in Allison Street, very near the Southern police station in Craigie Street and, as the robbers were carrying the three suitcases into the close, a police car returning from patrol passed by. The two officers in the car knew nothing of the robbery that had just taken place in Linwood, but one of them, Inspector Hyslop, had long suspected Wilson of being involved in the resetting of stolen goods and on impulse decided to investigate the contents of the three suitcases. Because of his police background Wilson was acquainted with Hyslop and his colleague, Constable Sellars. They had now been joined by three other beat men, Constables McKenzie, Barnett and Campbell, who were on their way back to the station to finish their shift. To allay suspicion, Wilson invited them all into the flat for a festive drink, and as he went into the kitchen for glasses, Inspector Hyslop opened one of the suitcases and discovered wads of banknotes held together with paper bands marked 'Clydesdale Bank'.

The five policemen now began searching the house.. Wilson ran into the bedroom where he had left his gun, seized it and fired at Inspector Hyslop, who attempted to grapple with him. Fired at close range, the bullet hit the inspector on the side of the face, and he fell to the ground, still conscious, but paralysed from the impact. Hearing the shot, Detective McKenzie ran into the room and was shot in the head as he entered. The same fate befell Barnett as he too ran to investigate the shots. He fell dead. McKenzie was still alive, but Wilson put the pistol to his head and finished him off with a bullet. A postmortem was later to show that he could have lived had it not been for the second shot. Wilson then turned on Constable Sellars, who managed to escape the gunman by barricading himself in the bathroom.

As luck would have it, he was carrying one of the newly-issued portable two-way radios, and with it he was able to summon help. Wilson, in the meantime, was trying to force the bathroom door open to get at the policeman inside, but at this point Inspector Hyslop had regained some movement in his arms and grabbed him by the legs in an attempt to bring him down. Wilson turned the pistol to shoot at the inspector, but before he could fire at him again, Constable Campbell seized his chance and hit him with a flying tackle. A tussle ensued and Campbell was able to wrench the gun away and subdue the murderer. The place was soon flooded with police, and Wilson, together with his accomplice Sim, who had stood by motionless and fearful during all this mayhem, were marched off to the cells in the nearby station. Donaldson, who had fled at the first sight of the uniformed men, gave himself up some hours later.

At his trial Wilson was represented by Nicholas Fairbairn QC and tried by Lord Grant. He was sentenced to 25 years in prison and his accomplices were given 12 years each. He was lucky. The death penalty had been abolished just 12 months before.

A story that has been impossible to authenticate and may well be apocryphal, concerns a constable who worked a beat in the south side of the city in the immediate postwar years, a man of expensive tastes, strong appetites and doubtful honesty.

It is to be supposed that there never has been a constable in Glasgow, or anywhere else in the world for that matter, who has never partaken of some of the freely available perks of the job: the odd cup of tea or coffee and a wee heat and perhaps a meal in the back shop of some café or restaurant on his beat, a nip of whisky left for him in a neighbouring pub, or a bottle of Johnny Walker from a grateful shopkeeper whose premises he has secured when left unsafe. All of these practises are perhaps frowned upon in the police code of conduct, but they are hardly mortal sins that require condemnation.

But the policeman in question's behaviour was anything but venial. As the stories have it, he actively collaborated with criminals, specifically with a safe blower who plied his trade on the constable's beat. Once suitable targets had been identified, the safe blower would go about his business while the constable stood watch outside, and then the spoils would be divvied up. You might wonder why the alarm was not immediately raised by some neighbour on hearing the sound of the explosion, but the fact is that an experienced safe blower made very little noise in the course of a robbery.

Small shopkeepers did not make use of massive safes, and very little explosive was required to blow open the type usually encountered in the course of these thefts. Furthermore, the sound of the explosion would be completely muffled by the heavy blanket which the thief had wrapped round the safe and which formed part of the equipment carried for the job.

One night, a particularly tempting target presented itself in the shape of a tobacconist's shop. As usual, whilst his partner in crime worked away inside, the policeman stood guard. The safe blower suddenly appeared beside him. The battery of his torch had failed and he asked for the use of the constable's in order to finish the job. The torch was duly handed over, and when the safe blower had finished, the two separated, with the policeman going back to his beat and the burglar to his home. Later on in the night, to his horror, the constable noticed that he was minus a torch: had his partner taken it with him or had it been left in the burgled premises? He sweated out his shift and at the end of it did not go home, as he normally would have done, but waited impatiently until the morning arrival of the shopkeeper. The shopkeeper entered his premises, closely followed by the PC, ostensibly to make a purchase, and he shared in the shopkeeper's dismay at the discovery of the blown safe. Being a policeman, he immediately took charge of the situation, instructed the shopkeeper to phone his headquarters and whilst the owner was thus engaged he thankfully pocketed the missing torch, which he had spotted at the side of the burgled safe.

According to the myth, for myth it must surely be, his partnership with the safe blower lasted some time and was never discovered, but he was eventually dismissed from the force for persistent drunkenness whilst on duty.

Dangers

The dangers that constantly faced the man on the beat can perhaps be illustrated by the following examples:

One night in October 1953 a beat in the Garngad area was being patrolled by a Constable ———, a young rookie who had just finished his probationary period, and who had been assigned to that district a few weeks earlier. The area was notorious for its gangs of young hooligans and was normally patrolled in twos, but his companion had gone to accompany a stabbing victim to the hospital and was to have joined him later. The young constable, an immensely strong ex-serviceman with wartime commando experience, was in the process of checking shop premises, a procedure that had to be carried out twice on each shift. As he approached a row of some single storey shops he noticed movement and lights in one of them. He drew his baton and approached cautiously. The door of the shop was slightly ajar and as he drew close two men appeared from inside the premises, each carrying a sack of stolen articles. They responded to his challenge by charging at him full pelt, only to be laid low by two blows from his baton. Unknown to him, however, a third man had been standing as lookout on the low roof of the shop, and as the constable drew out his whistle to summon assistance, this man jumped down on the young rookie's head, kicking down with all his strength as he did so. The police helmet absorbed the full impact of the blow, but the constable was slammed into the ground, semi-stunned, but still able to wield his baton and lash out at his attacker, who had fallen to the pavement beside him. The blow smashed the man's knee and as the hooligan lay screaming on the ground the constable became aware that his own legs were paralysed and that he had no movement from the waist down. Though completely devoid of movement in his lower body, he was still able to blow his whistle and this he did incessantly, stopping only from time to time to subdue his three prisoners with blows from his baton as they stirred on the pavement beside him.

The repeated blasts from the whistle finally carried to the ears of two policemen on a neighbouring beat, and when they arrived at the scene they found the young rookie with his helmet jammed down on his head, sitting propped up against the wall of the shop and unable to move his legs. Three unconscious prisoners lay at his feet, and surrounding the four was a hostile crowd who had been attracted by the commotion, yelling abuse at the injured policeman who lay semi-paralysed and spitting defiance at them.

The policeman was taken to hospital where he lay for three weeks recovering from the injuries his spine had received from the impact of the hooligan's boots on his head. It was the opinion of the doctors who treated him that a lesser man would have been killed by such a blow. He returned to his duties some weeks later, with only a permanently slightly stiff neck to show for his experience, his confidence as high as ever and his ability to deal with the neds unimpaired.

The same constable tells of another incident that he was invloved in some years later:

> Big John and I were called to an incident in Stevensons Taylor's pub, remember the big pub at the corner of Parly Road and Buchanan Street? Well, some neds had been causing trouble and one of the barmen gave us a whistle. So in we go and we see a fella standing with a bad cut on his face and a barman trying to stop the blood. We sort things out and grabbed the two blokes who had done it and Big John takes the two neds out to

leave them in the box and come back to get statements. He's no away a minute when another fight starts and I grab one of the blokes who's waving a bottle and I stand with him with my back to a door at the back of the pub. Suddenly the door opens and a bloke comes out and stabs me in the back with something. I had to let go of the ned I was holding and when I was trying to turn round I get another stab, in the side this time, a real bad one, and I go down on my knees.

Funny thing about getting stabbed like that, you don't feel any pain at first, you just suddenly go weak, the pain starts after. Anyhow, there was a fella standing at the bar watching all this and when he sees the bloke's gonny stab me a third time he picks up a screw-top and smashes the ned's face in with it. They had to wire his face bones together at the Royal after. Well, the fella that saved me was a ned from the Garscube Road. John Foy his name was, a real hard man he was, him and his pal O'Hara called themselves 'The Kings of the Garscube Road'. I had pulled him in dozens of times at pitch and toss schools. If it wasn't for him the bloke in the pub would have done for me. OK, Foy was a ned, but there's neds and neds, you get the evil neds who'll do in old men and women for their pensions and use razors and knives, and you get the others who've got a half-decent streak in them and wouldn't harm old people. Years later I was in that pub checking it out and I saw John Foy standing at the bar with his wife. He had been going straight for a long time and I remembered he had saved me once, so I stood him and his wife a drink. The barman didn't want any money for it, they didn't take money for drink from the polis, but I said no way, this one I want to pay for.

One November night in 1962, Constable John Gunn was patrolling the area at the corner of Shamrock Street and Scott Street, engaged in checking that the shops along his beat were all properly secure. Hearing the smashing of glass, he ran to investigate and on turning the corner into Scott Street, he saw a figure standing in front of a shattered pub window. He approached cautiously and as he tapped the individual on the shoulder the man turned swiftly and as quick as a flash plunged a knife into the constable's chest. John Gunn grappled with his assailant, but was stabbed four more times until he fell weakened by loss of blood. His life was saved by a woman who happened to be walking on the other side of the road at the time. She rushed to his side as he lay on the ground, blew frantically on his whistle until another policeman appeared and staunched the flow of blood from his wounds until an ambulance appeared. The attacker was never traced.

Danger exists even when the policeman is off duty, when he can be the target for revenge attacks by hooligans bearing a grudge. In April 1969, Special Constable George Gates had occasion to bring about the arrest of three youths on a charge of attempted shopbreaking. The youths, who already had several convictions for the same offence on their records, were sentenced to some months in jail, and on being led away to prison were heard to make threats against the constable. In November of the same year, as he walked near his home in Hamiltonhill, he was attacked by three assailants and sustained fatal wounds from a meat cleaver wielded by one of the men. The killers, who in this case were arrested and charged with murder, were the three youths he had arrested earlier in the year.

∗   ∗   ∗

PC James Stewart, who patrolled the Garngad beat out of St Rollox station had the reputation of being one of the biggest and hardest men on the beat. His first name was unknown to all but his closest friends; he was simply known as 'Big Hitler', a nickname whose origins were obvious to any ned who ever came into contact with him, for he was merciless to the hooligans he had to confront on a daily basis. His ruthless approach to lawbreakers and the severity with which he handled them made him scores of enemies, and one day a group of neds decided to do away with him permanently. They climbed on to the roof of a tenement where some heavy iron gratings had been placed and loosened one from its moorings. They pushed it to the edge of the roof and as he was about to pass underneath, let it drop.

They had not judged the fall well, however, for the heavy grating smashed into the pavement about six feet in front of Big Hitler, knocking a chunk out of the cement. The startled policeman looked up, saw five heads peering over the roof of the three storey tenement, drew his baton, charged into the close and up the stairs and met the five hooligans on one of the landings. He laid the five of them low with blows from his baton and then summoned help with blasts from his whistle. The help was for the five would-be murderers, for they had to be taken to hospital by ambulance suffering from multiple injuries.

This is an account of Big Hitler as told by one of his contemporaries:

There were some tough beat police there, maybe not too much brain, but brave with plenty of brawn, which was what was needed. Best example was Big Hitler, Stewart his name was, who worked out of the St Rollox station. We used to take the mickey out of Big Hitler, because of his size and strength, but he used to take the mickey back out of the rest of us. To show you how strong he was. One day at the Normal School, at the corner of New City Road and the Cowcaddens, the school gate fell on top of a wee girl. He was on the school crossing close by at the time. He heard people screaming and he rushed and lifted the gate off the girl without breaking sweat. It must have weighed hundredweights, because later on it took three men to shift it. Can you imagine him coming at you with a baton? He was merciless with the neds and used to run them in black and blue. You know the story of the grating that was dropped on him on his beat in the Garngad? He nearly killed those five neds. They all walked backwards with a limp when they came out of hospital. He was a real brute of a man. When all's said and done though, he maybe wasn't a likeable chap, not like Big Alec, who was as strong as he was, maybe even stronger, and as brave and as tough with the neds, but a real nice guy, nice with it and plenty of brains too.

Big Hitler had a sense of humour, though, in his own way, a bit twisted maybe. I mentioned about him taking the mickey out of some of our men. For example, there was a polis called Charlie on the beat. This fella Charlie hated bookies. For some unknown reason he had a pathological hatred of them and shooed the runners off the streets at every oppor-tunity. Hitler and another bloke, McKeeve, they

Outside the Northern Police Station, Maitland Street, circa 1955.

Veteran constable with one of the first policewomen on the beat, circa 1974.

Policemen controlling a crowd at Hampden Park, 1955.

Pointsman at the junction of Renfrew Street and Hope Street, circa 1955. The blue
police box on the left, outside the Savoy Café, is the one referred to in this book.

Ex-servicemen march in George Square, 1956.

Glasgow Police tug-of-war team. Winners of the Paris International Exhibition
and the Scottish National Sports, 1889.

Begging—under 16 years.

Betting, transaction with young person—under 18 years (apparently).

Betting, on tracks—under 18 years.

Brokers, purchasing from—under 16 years (apparently).

Brothels, children in—4 to 16 years.

Burning, unprotected grate—child under 7 years.

Child—Definition C. & Y.P. Act, 1937—under 14 years.

Chimney Sweep—21 years.

Collections, house to house collectors or street collectors—16 years.

Consent—Sexual Acts—16 years.

Criminal Responsibility, age of—8 years.

Cruelty (a) to Child—16 years.
       (b) overlaying—under 3 years.
       (c) liquor to child—under 5 years.

Dancing Partner, girl—18 years (condition of licence).

Dangerous Performance—
    (a) public—16 years.
    (b) training—12 years.
    (c) training under licence—12 to 16 years.

Dealers (old metal and marine stores), purchase—under 16 years (apparently).

Driving Licence—
    (a) motor cycle—16 years.
    (b) motor car—17 years.
    (c) P.S.V./H.M.V.—21 years.

8

Drunk, in charge of child—under 7 years (apparently).

Employment—
    (a) child—15 years.
    (b) child under licence—13 to 15 years.
    (c) licensed premises—18 years.
    (d) street trading—18 years.

Exciseable liquor—
    (a) consumption at Bar—under 18 years.
    (b) purchasing at Bar—under 18 years.
    (c) present at Bar—under 14 years.
    (d) sell to child (except in sealed bottle)—under 14 years.

Explosives, sale—under 13 years (apparently).

Firearms—
    (a) gift or borrowed—under 14 years.
    (b) purchase or hire—under 17 years.

Fireworks, sale—under 13 years (apparently).

Methylated Spirits, sale—14 years.

Pawnbroker—
    (a) employee—16 years.
    (b) take pledge—under 14 years.

Pedlar—over 17 years.

School Age—compulsory, 15 (power to raise to 16).

Sexual Acts—consent—16 years.

Shebeen—Child: 4-16 years.

Street Trading—18 years.

Tobacco, sale to—under 16 years (apparently).

Window Cleaner (business)—18 years.

Window Cleaning (perform)—17 years.

Young Persons—Definition, C. & Y.P. Act, 1937—14-17 years.

9

Pages from an Aide Memoire for beat constables, circa 1946. In this booklet: 'The aspects of Police Duty selected for inclusion are those which are most likely to confront a beat Constable.'

(13) **Eyebrows**—colour, thick, thin, bushy, plucked, arched, meet in centre, sparse.

(14) **Eyes**—colour, cast, blind, missing, glass, red-rimmed, long lashes, wears spectacles (for reading or habitually: horn-rimmed, pince-nez, bi-focal, shape of lens or frame), eyelids droop.

(15) **Nose**—large, small, long, short, hooked, irregular, turned-up, Roman, Jewish, broken, bulbous, broad base, wide or narrow nostrils.

(16) **Mouth**—large, small, habitually open, close-shut.

(17) **Lips**—thick, thin, loose, hare-lip, well shaped, upper or lower protrudes.

(18) **Teeth**—clean, discoloured, decayed, widely spaced, irregular, overlap, dentures, fillings, gaps, gold-crowned, toothless.

(19) **Chin**—dimpled, cleft or double, pointed, round, protrudes, recedes, square jaw.

(20) **Ears**—large, small, protrude, cauliflower, lobeless, large lobes, pierced.

(21) **Hands**—long, short, broad, long fingers, short fingers, well kept, rough. **Nails**—long, short, bitten, dirty, manicured, varnished (colour).

(22) **Voice**—accent, gruff, melodious, high-pitched, deep, loud, soft, effeminate, affected, lisp, stammer, or other impediment, difficulty in pronouncing certain words or letters.

(23) **Marks, Deformities, etc.**—(Especially those visible or on forearms—commence at top of head and work downwards)—scars, birth-marks, moles, freckles, tattoos, deformities, amputations, limp.

(24) **Unusual Features**—mannerisms (such as strokes nose or ear), nervous cough, habitually uses a particular phrase or phrases, peculiar walk (rolling, swinging, slouching), speaks of some particular part of the world or country, of rich relatives, experience, prowess at games, accomplishments (plays piano or other instrument, performs conjuring tricks or acrobatic feats), smokes (if a pipe, shape or make, gold or silver bands, brands of tobacco; if cigarettes, brand, chain-smoker, makes own, peculiar manner of holding it); drinks beer, wine or spirits—favourite brand; associates with prostitutes; takes snuff.

(25) **Wearing Apparel**—description of clothing worn.

(26) **Places Frequented**—dance halls (good or low-class), greyhound race tracks, steeple-chase courses, flat race courses, pony-trotting courses, dirt tracks, billiard saloons, type of public house—any particular bar, class of hotel—uses lounge or bar.

(27) Descriptions of suspects should be as detailed as possible.

(28) Peculiarities are very important.

(29) Mention if a disguise may be used.

(30) Photographs and specimens of handwriting should be obtained if available.

(31) Arrange description under the headings shown. Descriptive terms given are merely suggestions and should be altered or added to as required.

20

21

manufactured a bookie, invented him. There was a publican at the corner of Dalhousie Sreet and New City Road very pally with Hitler. One day, when Charlie was due to pass the pub door, Hitler got the publican to appear with a wad of money and start giving it out to Hitler, saying 'this is so-and-so's winnings, and this is so-and-so's winnings, will you see that they get it, and this is a wee bung for yourself'. Charlie nearly went daft at this, and started looking for this bookie to arrest him, creeping up closes in Cambridge Street for days looking for the non-existent bookie until we told him. He never forgave Hitler.

Then there was the Ibrox incident. Hitler was a great Rangers man and not too fond of the Celtic, to put it mildly. They used to say that at Old Firm games all the bodies he chucked into the Black Marias wore green scarves and that he never arrested anyone wearing a blue one. He was always posted at the Celtic end at the Old Firm games and this day it was near the end of the match and Celtic were winning one–nil. Suddenly with about a minute to go Rangers equalised and Hitler went daft, he took off his helmet and whirled it round his head with the strap. These straps weren't very strong, they were designed that way in case some ned tried to strangle you with the helmet from behind, and it snapped and the helmet flew off into the Celtic crowd and was never seen again. That was great for the Celtic fans, getting a police helmet as a memento and he nearly went daft yelling at the crowd who had nicked his helmet. He would have arrested them all if he could. Hitler got a roasting from the higher-ups for that one and he never got back to a Celtic–Rangers game.

Right enough, he was a real blue-nose, but he could take a joke about it. All the beat men used to go into the back shop of the Savoy for a break, a cup of tea, a smoke or a plate of chips or something. There was a box at the Hope Street door of the place and it was handy. One of the waitresses who served him got hold of a plate with a picture of the Pope on it and served him up a fish supper on it. He never said a word and finished it off. The next time he went in there was another girl on and she gave him a supper on an ordinary plate. He said, 'Where's the plate with the Pope? The chips tasted better off it!'

But he was Rangers daft. On Saturday afternoons, after losing his helmet, instead of doing duty at the matches, he was always given the Cambridge Street–Renfrew Street points duty. Saturday afternoons were always dead quiet in the city centre then, everybody was away at the matches and there was absolutely nothing doing at the points, maybe a car every half-hour or so. One Saturday there was a Rangers–Celtic match on at Ibrox and Big Hitler was standing at the points doing nothing. So he goes to the Hope Street box and puts on a long raincoat and takes the subway at the Cowcaddens down to Ibrox and nips in when the match had started. A guy comes up and stands beside him, and when they look at one another they both got a fright. It was an inspector he knew and he wisnay supposed to be there either! But he was a great beat man, none better, he kept the neds in their place and you were safe to go about your business on his beat.

Big Hitler makes me think about the nicknames some of the lads had. Most of them were spot-on and suited the guy down to a T. We had 'Tadger',

'Mickey Mouse', 'The Ghoul', 'Abie', 'The Flea', 'Grubber', 'The Wolf', 'Big Farty', 'Tom Mix', 'The Louse', 'Sorrowful', and 'Pedro'.

Funny thing, I can remember the nicknames, but don't ask me to remember what their real names were!

Danger of severe bodily harm could come from sources other than human.

One day early in January 1951, newly promoted Detective Constable Joe Beattie was on his way to give evidence at a trial at Glasgow Sheriff court. The promotion to the CID had come after only four years on the beat, where his diligence and application had brought him to the attention of his superiors. It was his first case as a detective and it was to signal the start of a very successful career in the CID, a career which might never have started had the following incident come off badly for him, as it might well have.

He was about to enter the court when he heard crashing noises and shouts behind him. He turned and a few yards away he saw a huge carthorse rearing up on its hind legs and kicking out at a barking dog in front of it. The horse was pulling a loaded cart and, as the carter tried to get the horse under control, it threw him to the ground and stampeded along the busy Ingram Street, with the cart shedding its load as it careered behind the frightened horse. Joe sprinted after the animal, caught its reins and was dragged 200 yards along the street before he could get the animal under control. Luckily, despite being bruised and battered by the impact of lampposts and parked cars, he was not seriously injured. The only thing was that his shoes had been literally torn from his feet by the cobblestones as he was dragged along, and another pair had to be found for him before he could continue on his way to the court. He was heard to say afterwards that it was a toss-up as to who was the more frightened, him or the horse!

He asked the railway authorities for compensation for his shoes and received a following letter, part of which is reproduced below.

J. Beattie Esq   13th February 1952
16 Grafton Square
GLASGOW G1

Dear Sir,
I am in receipt of your letter of the 7th February and note it will not be possible for you to call in at my Office until after the 16th current.

Your action in stopping the runaway horse is much appreciated and in order to settle your claim for damage to your shoes, I am willing to make you a payment of £2.10.0d.

Stopping runaway horses seemed to be a fairly common occurrence then, for only two years before, five officers, John Stewart, William Cook, Stanley Moon, Ron Winkworth, and W McDowall were all awarded the Glagow Corporation Medal for Bravery for subduing runaway horses in or near the city centre.

Attempting to play the good Samaritan can have its unexpected dangers too. One day, at the time when tramcars still ran up and down Hope Street, off-duty Constable McArthur was about to cross the road in the vicinity of Sauchiehall Street when his attention was drawn by shouts and screams from some distance away. He ran to investigate and saw that a pedestrian had been run over by a northbound tram and lay jammed on top of the 'cowcatcher' platform carried by all the older trams as standard equipment. The man, heavily built and seemingly in his twenties, was unconscious and was trapped well under the body of the tram. There was no visible injury. Each tram carried jacking equipment and with this the front of the tram was raised slightly to allow PC McArthur to crawl under in an attempt to release the trapped man. The man's jacket had become snagged up in the wooden slats of the cowcatcher and, try as he might, the constable could not drag the heavy body out. By this time the two beat policemen had arrived on the scene and one of them handed McArthur a large kitchen knife, borrowed from a nearby restaurant, so that the impeding jacket could be cut away and the man released. McArthur, who was off-duty and in civilian clothes, hacked away at the jacket and finally was able to drag the heavy body from under and having done so, stood up, still clutching the heavy kitchen knife in his hand. The man on the ground opened his eyes and fixed them on his rescuer, who spoke reassuringly to him, telling him that an ambulance was on its way and that everything would be all right. Without uttering a word, eyes firmly fixed on his saviour, the man leapt to his feet, delivered a stunning head-butt to the face of the astonished McArthur and ran off along the pavement, leaving the shattered policeman behind with blood streaming from a broken nose. The two equally astonished uniformed men gave chase and grappled with the man who stopped struggling as soon as he saw the uniforms, still without uttering a single word.

He was a deaf-mute, could hear nothing of what was being said and had no recollection of having been hit by a tram. He knew only that something had happened to render him unconscious, and that when he came to he was minus his jacket and that a man holding a knife was standing over him and threatening him with it. In self-defence, since he assumed that the man with the knife had attacked him and stolen his jacket and was the cause of him having lost consciousness, he defended himself in the only way he could and then had tried to run away!

A year or so before this incident, the same constable was involved in another dangerous event, this time however, being saved from potential danger by the intervention of a member of the public.

Saturday was always a busy day for the cinemas in Glasgow, and as usual there was a long queue waiting at the amphitheatre entrance to the New Savoy picture house in Renfrew Street. Patrolling the beat there on that afternoon, Constable McArthur saw the queue suddenly scatter and heard screams coming from the vicinity of the pay box. A man in sailor uniform was standing there with a large knife in his hand, slashing at the empty air around him and making threatening motions with it to anyone within range. He seemed to be either drunk or drugged or both, and McArthur, drawing a deep breath, drew his baton and approached.

'Drop that knife!'

He shouted, more in hope than in expectation that the man would do as he was told. But now, a target identified, the man focused on the policeman and made towards him with the threatening blade.

Sitting in the nearby Savoy, eating a fish supper, was a regular customer there, Sandy McKenzie, one-time light-heavyweight boxing champion of Scotland. He had sat watching the happenings across the road, and as the policeman approached to tackle the knife-wielding sailor, he stepped into the road beside him.

'Gie us a wee bit room,' he said to the constable, pushing him aside with one hand. He went up to the man, ducked under the slashing knife and delivered a powerful blow to the solar plexus. Gasping for air, the sailor dropped the knife, and as he doubled up in pain, Sandy finished him off with a smashing blow to the side of the jaw.

'Couldnay havum cuttin' up the polis,' he remarked to the astonished McArthur, and went back to his unfinished fish supper. The constable, in recounting the story, said that he had never been so relieved in all his life !

In July 1969 a brutal murder had been committed in the town of Ayr. During one night two men had burgled the home of an elderly couple, Mr and Mrs Ross, and had beaten and tortured them in an attempt to have them divulge the combination of their safe. As a result of the beating Mrs Ross died, and suspicion fell on a well-known criminal, Paddy Meehan, who was known to have been in that region of Ayrshire with a companion on the night of the murder. The truth of the matter, which did not come to light until much later, was that the perpetrators of the murder were two other notorious evil-doers, Tank McGuiness and Ian Waddell.

Paddy Meehan had a perfect alibi for the Ross murder. At the very time when the elderly couple were being beaten up in their home in Ayr, he and an accomplice, James Griffiths, were breaking into a motor taxation office in Stranraer. Faced with a charge of murder, Meehan decided to tell the police what he was actually doing that night and gave the name of his partner in crime as corroboration. At that time James Griffiths lived in an attic flat in Holyrood Crescent, a quiet street off Great Western Road. Five detectives drove to the address to question him about Meehan's alibi, parked the car in the street under his flat, climbed up the four flights of stairs and knocked on the suspect's door.

It was immediately thrown open, and there stood Griffiths with a shotgun pointing at their heads. Since they were unarmed, they ducked low and beat a hasty retreat, crouching down to avoid the shots now being fired at them by Griffiths. One of the detectives was slightly wounded in the back, and as they arrived back at the car parked in the street below, they were greeted by a fusillade of shots from the attic window, this time by a rifle. Whilst they were diving for cover on the far side of the vehicle, a bullet sliced off the heel of one of the policemen's shoes.

Given the criminal history of James Griffiths, they ought not to have been quite so casual in their approach, for the man had a long list of convictions for various violent crimes. These included armed robbery, fraud and assault, and he had the doubtful distinction of being one of the few prisoners ever to have escaped from Parkhurst prison on the Isle of Wight. What they could not have known, however, was that on the day in question Griffiths was high on drugs and had been taking strong doses of Benzedrine tablets, all of which had brought to the fore and pumped up his natural aggressiveness.

Not content with firing at the men who had come to question him, Griffiths continued his shooting, this time picking as targets any pedestrian who happened to be passing on the pavements below. He fired rapidly and haphazardly, and before the street could be sealed off by the dozens of policemen who had arrived at the scene, his bullets had wounded seven passing civilians. He seemed to have a limitless supply of ammunition, for when finally he had no more human targets to fire at he continued shooting, this time choosing random targets amongst the numerous cars parked in the street below. The shooting finally stopped, and the police marksmen who had arrived at the scene and had surrounded the flat waited tensely for the next move by the gunman.

Unknown to them, by this time Griffiths, loaded down with a rifle, a shotgun and two bandoliers of ammunition, had made good his departure from the flat via a back door and was running away down a side street. He stepped in front of an approaching car, forced it to stop, then shot the driver, dragged him out from behind the steering wheel and drove off as far as the Round Toll, where Garscube Road merges into Maryhill Road. There he stopped the car and ran madly into the pub at the corner, the Round Toll Bar. By this time his escape had been discovered by the police, the stolen car had been followed and every available police vehicle was directed to where he now was.

There were half a dozen or so customers in the pub when Griffiths crashed in. He slammed his assortment of weapons on to the bar and demanded whisky.

As he drank some out of a bottle, his attention was taken by an old newsvendor who was standing at the end of the bar, open-mouthed at the spectacle. Griffiths picked up a rifle and without warning shot the old man dead. He then menaced the terrified drinkers at the bar with his guns, but instead of shooting someone else, he gathered the rest of his weapons, ran out into the street, jumped into a passing lorry, and ordered the driver at gunpoint to drive him to Springburn. The police cars had not yet arrived at the pub, but a passing beat man commandeered a taxi and had the driver follow, radioing in the lorry's progress as they went. Griffith stopped the lorry at Kay Street in Springburn, ran into a close and up the stairs to the top storey, where he managed to force an entry into one of the flats. From this vantage point he again began to fire haphazardly at pedestrians in the street below, stopping only when the police converged on the area and sealed off the road.

Chief Superintendent Finlayson and Sergeant Smith, two of the armed police contingent, waited until the firing had stopped and began to move slowly up the final flight of steps to the door of the flat where Griffiths lay waiting. They got to the door and Finlayson, kneeling down with gun at the ready, slowly opened the letter box flap and peered inside. Griffiths heard the slight noise at the door, wheeled and fired. Finlayson, his gun already through the letter box, got his shot off first and his bullet took Griffiths high in the chest. Griffiths fired again as he was falling to the floor but his shot went wild. He died as he was being carried to the ambulance. In the course of his mad rampage he had killed one man and wounded 13 others.

There is a rather sad epilogue to the story. A week or so after these events Griffiths' mother wrote a pathetically worded letter to the police. In it she expressed her sorrow at her son's actions, and told the policeman who had killed him not to worry too much about it, because her son was 'a really bad man'.

Without anyone to corroborate his alibi, Meehan was convicted of the murder of Rachel Ross and sentenced to a term in prison, despite his having named the two actual murderers, McGuiness and Waddell, at his trial. There were some who said that given his record he deserved to be in prison whether he had committed that particular crime or not, but in a sequence of bizarre events that would not be believed had they been part of a mystery novel, he was eventually exonerated.

Some time after the trial and sentencing of Meehan, Tank McGuiness was himself found murdered in a flat in Springfield Road.

His death freed his lawyer, Joe Beltrami, from the constraint of client-lawyer confidentiality, allowing him to report to the Lord Advocate that McGuiness had confessed to him that he and Ian Waddell had carried out the burglary and beatings at the Ross household and had thus murdered Rachel Ross.

On the basis of this the case was re-opened and after much legal manoeuvering Paddy Meehan was granted a royal pardon and released.

✳   ✳   ✳

If the detectives who had gone to question Griffiths had approached him rather too casually in the light of what happened, the same cannot be said of the men who went to arrest Walter Ellis one day in 1966. They were armed and ready for all eventualities and rightly so, for Ellis, one of the most dangerous criminals Glasgow has ever produced, was known to be armed, and was about to be arrested for participation in an armed robbery at a bank in Pollokshaws. Until that time, his long catalogue of crime had culminated in his arrest and trial for the murder of a taxi driver in the Castlemilk housing estate. In that case his defence was undertaken by the team of Beltrami and Fairbairn, and after a long and controversial trial, a verdict of not proven was returned, a verdict which said a lot for the skill of the defence team, for there was not a soul in Glasgow who did not believe Ellis to be guilty of the murder of the taxi driver.

The bank in Pollokshaws had been held up by three masked men and a sum in excess of £20,000 had been taken. The investigation was led by the famous Elphinstone Dalglish, and Ellis was identified as having led the gang. Since Ellis was notorious for his violence and was known to be carrying a gun, the squad sent to arrest him was fully armed and ready for any eventuality. They were under the command of Detective Inspector David McNee, the officer who was eventually to become Chief Constable of Glasgow, and later Chief of the London Metropolitan. Ellis lived in a cottage near Newton Mearns and early one morning the house was surrounded, the door smashed in with a battering-ram and Ellis was overpowered before he could blink an eye. No gun was found in the cottage, but a ticket to the left-luggage office in the Central railway station led the police to a suitcase in which they found several rounds of ammunition and the gun used in the robbery. He was sentenced to 21 years' imprisonment and was released after serving 14 of them.

Although in some stations the pay office was manned by a civilian, in the late forties and early fifties the one in the Northern was run by a Constable Sandy Fraser. Sandy, approaching his fifties and retirement, had been a beat man for the whole war period. Although he had satisfied the minimum requirement of five foot ten inches at the time of his joining the force, he was called 'Wee' Sandy by his mates. The reason for his appointment as a pay clerk was that he was going deaf, as the result of a blow to the head some years before, received during a night shift in the New City Road. As he was doing the usual tour of inspection of the backyards, a hooligan, possibly to pay off an old score, had lain in wait for him in a close, and smashed in his helmet with a blow from an iron bar. Another policeman saw the assailant running out of the close, brandishing the weapon, and Sandy was found by him, unconscious and bleeding profusely from a wound in the head. His stout helmet had saved his life, and he was able to return to duty after a few weeks, only to discover that his hearing had been affected and was rapidly becoming more and more impaired. Afraid of early retirement, with a consequent drop in pension, he did his best to hide his condition and it only became apparent to his colleagues one day when he answered some comments his mate on the beat seemed to making to him. The colleague was in fact only chewing a caramel! Sandy, seeing the motion of the lips, thought he was being spoken to and began to answer monosyllabically and thus his deafness was discovered. His sympathetic superiors, so that he could serve out his time and retire on full pension, offered him the post as pay clerk, which he filled until he retired.

In 1969 William Kerr was Chief Constable of the Dunbartonshire Constabulary and had brought to that office a wealth of experience and innovative ideas. With the spread of motoring and roads, criminal methods were changing. No longer was the bank robber, housebreaker or malefactor more or less confined to his own territory for safe hiding places for himself and his loot. Fast cars and fast roads made it possible for the criminal to easily put hundreds of miles between himself and the scene of his crime, and police investigations were made all the more difficult by this new factor.

William Kerr had given a lot of thought to this and had concluded that such new developments should be countered by others equally new and decided on the experiment of using helicopters as part of police equipment to combat crime. To assess the feasibility of such tactics, a helicopter trip round the Firth of Clyde was arranged for Kerr and some other senior officers, amongst whom was David McNee, the Glasgow Chief. At the end of the flight Kerr stepped out of the aircraft, moved back to allow his companions to descend and walked right into the helicopter's rotor blades. He was lucky not to have been killed outright, but his injuries were horrific. As a result he lost an eye and the use of an arm, and these disabilities put an end to his career. The idea of using helicopters in police work was put on hold, and was not considered again until the passage of many more years.

A Helping Hand

By many, especially the elderly, the man on the beat was regarded not only as someone who kept people under control, attended to accidents, directed traffic and supervised the school crossings, he was also considered a friend who could be turned to for help if the necessity should arise. An old, retired constable reminisces:

Right after the school crossing duty we had to go along to Killermont Street bus station to do traffic control there, to get the buses in and out of the place and keep traffic moving at busy periods. The bus station was in a very cramped area with narrow approach roads at the back, and at the rush hour with extra buses laid on and the traffic in the street at peak, things got jammed up unless we were there to sort things out. Big John and I were usually on duty in Buchanan Street, one of us guiding the buses out and the other one sorting out the traffic on the main road. Sometimes the weather was terrible and even if you had waterproofs and leggings you could get well soaked from the splashes from the puddles in the street.

There was an old woman lived three up in the Stevenson Taylor tenement next to the bus station. She spent her day looking out of the window and always gave us a wee wave when we came on duty. After we had finished she used to wave us up for a cup of tea and scones, although we weren't supposed to leave the beat for anything like that. Sometimes she gave us a bowl of hot soup. It was great, a real nice old biddy she was; she had lost a son in the war, and she looked after us well, Mrs Grant her name was. One day she asks us up, it had been a bitterly cold wet day and we were glad of the bowl of soup and the scone she had waiting for us.

She was a wee bit sad looking that day and didn't have much to say and we asked her what was wrong and she said that the stairs were getting a bit too much for her at her age and she had been on at the factor to get her a ground floor house. Well, he had got one for her, but it was two closes further up the street and although she already had the key she didn't have any money to do the flitting and she had to take the house right away or else it would go to somebody else. So we said, 'Don't you worry Ma, we'll shift the furniture for you,' and we started to shift the furniture down three stairs and through two back yards into her new house.

Sergeant Shanks couldn't find us on the beat and we hadn't put anything in the journal in the box, so he goes round to the bus station and he asks around and somebody told him we were up in Mrs Grant's, so does he not come up to see what we were doing there and he gives us a bollocking for not being on the beat. When he sees what we're doing he says, 'The quicker you're finished the quicker you'll be back on your beat,' and he starts to help too.

There was a certain chief superintendent in charge then, and he starts looking for the men on the beat, especially the sergeant and he can't find them. Somebody tells him where he thinks we are so he comes up to see what we're up to. He sees what we're doing and he looks hard and gives the three of us a real bad bollocking and then he says, 'Finish up as quick as you can and get back on the beat, you know full well you're no supposed to be off it. I should have you up on a report.'

Then he stops and looks about a bit and asks, 'Is there a pulley in the house? I'm an expert on pulleys.' And he takes the pulley in the kitchen down and puts it back up in Mrs. Grant's new house. So, four-handed, we finish quick and we get back on the beat. She couldn't thank us all enough.

One day a couple of weeks later Big John and Shanks and I are told to go up to Superintendent Curdy's office pronto. 'Christ!' I say to myself, 'another bollocking for something.' We were always getting a bollocking for something, bumping neds too hard and things like that. So we go in wondering what's up and when we get in Curdy doesn't say a word but throws a letter at us and tells us to read it. Mrs Grant had written to the chief constable, Robertson it was at the time, to thank the police for the help we had given her in the flitting. Curdy says, 'Do you two not have enough to do on the beat without doing flittings as well?'

But I think the chief was pleased at the letter, because he doesn't give us a bollocking like we expected

There is nothing more uninviting and bleak than a wet, cold and windy Sunday morning in the Cowcaddens with nothing much to do and the two constables of the previous story had just started their early shift on such a day with the prospect of eight miserable hours on the beat ahead of them. The only thing they were glad about was that they weren't on a night shift. No activity on a Sunday to hasten the passing of the hours, no Savoy back shop for a smoke and a cup of coffee, for the place closed on Sunday, as did every other place of entertainment or refreshment where they could normally have spent the odd few minutes in between checking shop doors, middens and backyards. The only refuge available to them was the kitchen of Ferrari's restaurant in Sauchiehall Street, for although the restaurant itself was closed, Sunday was when the staff cleaned and polished the various pots, utensils and worktops used in the previous week's business.

Fortified by a coffee and a smoke and by nothing stronger, the two emerged from Ferrari's and started on the first round of their beat. Nothing stronger, because the duo, despite having been known to bend other regulations on occasion, never took alcohol whilst on duty. They turned into Renfrew Street, bracing their shoulders against the strong wind and driving rain, and there by the side of the Pavilion theatre they saw a parked car, the only vehicle in sight.

A figure, dripping with rain, stood by it fumbling in a very suspicious manner at one of the wheels and the two immediately investigated. There was nothing sinister about the man's activities. The car, a hired vehicle, had a puncture, and the driver had been trying for some time and without success to loosen the wheel bolts. He introduced himself as a tourist from Canada about to start a tour of Scotland with his wife, who was sitting patiently in the passenger seat. He seemed to be well past middle age, and was plainly exhausted by his fruitless efforts in the wind and rain. One of the constables involved takes up the tale.

The poor bugger looked dead beat, soaked to the skin he was, so I say to Big John, 'Tell you what, you take him up to Ferrari's and get him dried out and I'll change the wheel and drive the car back to pick you up,' and I say to the Canadian, 'If that's OK by you sir'. So the bloke says, 'Fine, that's real big of you, much appreciated,' and off he goes with Big John back to Ferrari's.

Well, it took me a good while to get the wheel changed, the nuts were rusted solid, but I finally manage it, although I'm pretty soaked myself by this time, even with waterproofs, and I get in and turn the car round and all the time the bloke's wife is sitting waiting in the passenger seat. We get to Ferrari's and go into the kitchen, and there's Big John sitting drinking a coffee, and no bloke, but there's a bundle of clothes getting dried at a fireplace. The bloke's been shivering with the cold so the cook's told him to take his clothes off and go up to the staff room and take a hot shower.

The bloke comes down after five minutes in a big bath towel and drinks a cup of hot coffee and he and his wife can't thank us enough and offer to buy us a drink or something, but we say no thanks, we're way behind already, and we go up to the Hope Street box and mark the journal with an hour ago time which is when we should have marked it in the first place. So we go round the beat back to Ferrari's and the bloke and his wife are long gone, but he's left a fiver with the cook for drinks all round after the shift, which was just great, and we go back after and knock back a couple of doubles each.

About six weeks go by and we get called up to Curdy's office. We're wondering what's up and what have we done this time, but again he disnae say a word and throws a letter at us. Well, it turns out that the Canadian in the car is an assistant commissioner in the Saskatchewan police and he's written to the chief thanking him for all the help we had given him that morning, blah, blah, blah. Curdy looks at us. 'Christ,' he says, 'a couple of months ago you're helping with a flitting and now you're mechanics. Well, if you want to start looking for a permanent job in a garage you're going the right way about it. Get back to your bloody beat, the both of you!'

*   *   *

On Saturdays the shops in Sauchiehall Street, the Cowcaddens and the city centre in general had their busiest day of the week. It was also the day when professional shoplifters used to go about their business at a time when shoplifting was a serious crime on a par with housebreaking. Stealing from shops was a fairly difficult affair then and required a degree of skill, speed and nerve to carry out. In the shops and large department stores all merchandise was exhibited and sold over a counter by sales assistants and it was no easy thing to steal goods from right under their eyes. There was no-open plan layout of stock as there is in all the stores today and the only exposed goods were of small value, usually exhibited under a glass counter. Nowadays wares are displayed openly and with practically no protection and customers can touch and inspect merchandise without hindrance. Such a system is a happy hunting ground for the casual shoplifter, who can finger objects at their leisure and then pop an object into a bag or pocket with a fair chance of not being observed by a member of staff or by the ubiquitous TV eye.

Moreover, nowadays the impression conveyed to the potential thief in department stores is that he has a good chance of getting away with it, even if caught. The signs read, 'Thieves may be prosecuted', instead of the peremptory 'Shoplifters will be prosecuted'. In the immediate postwar years if the police were called in to answer a shoplifting call it would almost invariably end up with some person being charged with theft.

Invariably that is, unless the constables called to an

incident used their own discretion in the matter. One Saturday afternoon the light on the Hope Street box began to flash and was answered after a few minutes by the two constables on the beat, who were instructed to go immediately to a large Sauchiehall Street store nearby to investigate a reported shoplifting incident. One of the policemen involved tells this story:

> We went down right away to see what was up and when we got down to the store the assistant manager took us into his office. There was a young black fella there about 19 years of age and when he sees us he bursts out crying. We ask a few questions and it turns out he was in Glasgow to study at the university on a special government grant from Ghana and that he would be in big trouble if the people there got to know what he had done. He would get sent back to who knows what kind of punishment and he would be a disgrace to his family and it would be terrible for them. It turns out that he had taken a tin of boot polish and a shoe brush from a counter display. The two things added up to one and fourpence. So we looked at the young fella sitting there sobbing his eyes out and we looked at one another. So we get hold of the assistant manager and take him into a quiet corner and say to him, 'Just for a lousy one and fourpence worth – do you want us to put this chap in the cells for a night and maybe get him deported for theft or something and maybe ruin his life? It's up to you, do you want to be a bastard about it? We think this should be one of the ones you forget about.'
>
> I knew the assistant manager, Peter his name was, he was a decent enough bloke, so he looks at us looking hard at him and he shuffles his feet around a bit, then he says 'OK this time, but he needs a good talking to

at least.'

So we make the fella pay for what he'd taken, I don't know why he wanted to nick the things in the first place, he had plenty of money on him, and march him out and up the street into the Hope Street box and give him a real talking to, we put the fear of God in him, we do. We tell him he's a marked man now and if there is a next time he's in the calaboose for a year at least and he better not do anything like that again and then tell him to bugger off and he kisses our hand in gratitude. The manager of the store —— his name was, a real bastard he was, finds out about this, and does he not report us right away to the Super! Curdy didn't have a choice, it's an official complaint and he has to pass it on to the central office. So a day or two later Big John and I get hauled in front of the chief constable and we get the biggest roasting we ever had.

'Neglect of duty,' says the chief. 'No matter how little was involved, the law is the law and that was theft and you are in neglect of duty. You are not judges, you are policemen and you are sworn to uphold the law and what you have done is a dereliction of duty,' and he gets laid into us real hard. Big John usually never says much, but he got red around the ears as he listens to all this and he made the longest speech I ever heard him make.

'Sir, I've been a policeman on this beat for ten years and I've put as many neds behind bars as anyone, but I'm a man first, and I think it would have been a bloody shame to put that fella in the cells with the razor men and neds and the drunks and all for a lousy one and fourpence and I think maybe if you had got the case and if you had seen him and talked to him you would have done the same, sir.'

Robertson begins to get red around the ears too, and I'm waiting for him to explode and kick us out of the force or something but he sits still for a minute, looking at us and breathes hard then starts giving us a good talking to about duty and protecting the public and their property and stuff like that and we better not do anything like that again or else it's our job and sends us on our way.

Well, about 18 months later we get a call from the same shop. A man had been caught molesting a young girl in a stockroom. So we go down and who was the bloke caught with his hand up the lassie's knickers? The manager! So we march him up to the station and throw him into the cells. The girl refused to testify so the case never came to court, but the manager got the sack.

I tell you, I got more pleasure out of pulling him in than I would have got from sticking fifty bad neds in the cells.

The man on the beat would sometimes turn a blind eye to activities well outside the law, but perhaps, some might say, excusable in humanitarian terms. Sixty years ago for a young teenage or unmarried girl to become pregnant was the biggest disgrace that could befall her and her family, and backstreet abortionists, known as the 'wummen with the knitting needle' could earn many a quick shilling. These interventions were usually botched up affairs, carried out in primitive, unsanitary conditions, often leading to an emergency visit to the hospital and to disastrous health consequences for the poor unfortunate girl. Tales were legion of the deaths that had resulted from such backstreet abortions. If discovered, the 'wummen with the knitting needle'

were, without exception, severely dealt with by the courts.

On Sunday mornings the city centre was always empty and devoid of pedestrians, but on those days, in the Hope Street–Renfield Street area, you could be sure of seeing a few women, always in twos, apparently sauntering aimlessly up and down the street. They would disappear into a close in Weymss Street, to emerge 15 minutes or so later and then leave the scene quickly, heads lowered and with never a word exchanged.

This scene was enacted Sunday after Sunday, year after year, until suddenly in the early fifties, this traffic ceased. The tenement which housed the illegal abortion clinic was to be demolished to make way for the redevelopment of the Cowcaddens. The service was provided by a nurse from one of the Glasgow hospitals, expertly and in the cleanest conditions possible, completely free of charge. The nurse was motivated only by humanitarian considerations and a desire to keep the young women concerned out of the clutches of the backstreet abortionists. In all the years that these scenes were enacted there was never any police intervention. Either the men on the beat did not know what was going on under their noses, which was highly improbable, or their inactivity was a form of passive and humanitarian helping hand.

✳   ✳   ✳

An elderly couple came slowly arm in arm through the station doors and timidly and hesitatingly approached the bar. The duty officer lifted his glance from a pile of paperwork and observed them curiously. They both seemed to be in their seventies, and were small and neatly dressed. The woman's eyes were red and swollen with tears, the man's face etched with lines of worry.

'What can I do for you?'

The man coughed nervously and replied in an Italian accented voice, 'Please can you tell us where our son is? We were

111

on holiday in Rothesay when Italy declared war and we came home as soon as we could, but we found the shop all smashed and boarded up and our son is not at home and we are very worried.'

The duty officer gazed at the man impassively, went through a door and returned accompanied by a sergeant. Sergeant McKenzie was a grizzled veteran of World War I, tall and powerfully built, now about 50 years of age and very annoyed about the present war which had put paid to his ambition of an early retirement from the force. He towered over the anxious couple at the other side of the bar.

'Name?'

'My name is Togneri. My son is Peter and we are very worried about him. Can you find out what happened to him? He is not at home and has left no message for us.'

Sergeant McKenzie thought for a moment. He looked at the two old people and felt a vague stirring of pity for them. He supposed it wasn't their fault that Mussolini had seen fit to declare war on Britain a few hours before. He knew where Peter was. At that very moment he was sitting disconsolately in a cell a few feet away where he had put him two days before, in the company of five others, all apathetically awaiting their fate as Italian internees. He also knew all about their boarded-up shop. It was he who had called a local firm of joiners to have the place made secure after the damage inflicted by a rampaging mob on the night of Italy's declaration of war.

'I'm afraid I can't say where your boy is, but I'm sure he's all right. There were a lot of Italians arrested a couple of days ago, but you go home and don't worry, you'll get word about him soon. I'm sure he's all right.'

Two days later the couple appeared again at the police station and asked to see Sergeant McKenzie.

'Please, we haven't heard anything about our boy yet, can you please find out what has happened to him?'

This time the sergeant could answer truthfully, for Peter

had been taken away by the military that very morning.

'I'm sorry, I really don't know, but don't worry, you'll hear something soon. I'm sure he's all right.'

The old woman's eyes were redder than ever with tears and she spoke for the first time, with an accent even thicker than that of her husband

'It's terrible not to know where he is, if we just knew he was all right that would be enough. And there's the shop, if we do not pay the rent Peter will lose it, and we want to have it ready for him when he comes back. We don't know what to do, we don't know who to talk to. Can we open it up again?'

The sergeant looked at her in amazement. The shop had been gutted just about a week ago by a mob and here was this wee woman ready to start it up again for the sake of her son. God alone only knew if she would ever see her boy again. The world was in flames, the Germans had taken over France and might invade at any minute and this wee woman was worried about paying the rent for her son's shop. The pity within him grew.

'Now you go home and don't worry, Mrs Togneri. Your boy is going to be all right, but I don't think you should try to open up the shop, not for a while yet anyhow. But if you're worried about it, I'll tell you what I'll do. I'll see if I can get somebody to fix it up for you and then you can decide if you want to open up again.'

His shift finished, the sergeant walked the short distance from the station to the Togneri shop and unlocked the padlock, which secured the repaired door. The key had been left in the station by the joiner who had been called out to make the ruined shop secure and as yet had not been handed over to the factor. The internal damage was worse than he had imagined it would be. Once a tidy café with ornate showcases for sweets and choco- lates, the place lay in ruins. Showcases were smashed, the counter hacked by blows from some heavy, sharp instrument, probably an axe, wall mirrors lay in shards of splintered glass, and the café had been stripped of all its stock of cigarettes and chocolates. The counter ice-cream freezer had been filled with an evil-smelling brown mixture with the consistency of mud.

The sergeant walked another short distance to the Togneri house and rapped on the door.

'Does your son have insurance on the shop?'

The anxious father produced a bundle of documents and handed them to the sergeant.

'Well, he's insured, but I don't know whether he's covered for this sort of thing. You go to this address,' he handed over the address of the joiner who had done the boarding up, 'tell him I sent you, tell him to get the place cleaned out and to come and see me.'

He cut short the stammered thanks and pre-empted the expected question.

'No, I don't know where your son is, but don't worry, he's all right, I'm sure.'

Under the discrete supervision of the sergeant the shop was soon back in reasonable condition, windows replaced, new door installed and wooden shelving put in place of the smashed glass originals. He gruffly rejected the Togneri's fulsome thanks.

'Do you really want to open the place up again? OK, go ahead, but close as soon as it gets dark. If all you want to do is pay the rent that should give you enough drawings with a wee bit over.'

By this time the old couple had received news of their son. He was alive and well and very lucky. He had survived the sinking of the ill-fated *Arandora Star* and after a series of vicissitudes had found himself an internee in Australia, where the Government in its wisdom had decided to send several groups of Italian enemy aliens. The two old parents were enemy aliens too, but fortunately had not been included in the arrests, and so they were left to sell what goods they could in a time of war, shortage and rationing so that the business could be kept going for the return of their interned son.

This they did under the unobtrusive supervision of Sergeant McKenzie. He paid them a daily visit, showing himself off to the locals, who were thus given fair warning that the two old folk enjoyed his protection. For four years this procedure continued, the sergeant helping the two in any way he could, always sternly refusing any form of gift or remuneration, and once dramatically blowing his nose with a large hankerchief when informed by the local priest that old Mrs Togneri had a monthly Mass said at the church for the good intentions of Sergeant McKenzie. The procedure with a handkerchief was probably enacted to hide the policeman's embarrassment, for he was not Catholic.

The war finished, all prisoners were released and internees allowed to return home, but all the old people's efforts and sacrifices for the sake of their son Peter, and the sergeant's efforts on behalf of Peter's parents, proved to be in vain, for at war's end Peter elected to remain and shape his future in Australia. The old Togneris closed the little shop, sadly took their leave of the policeman who had befriended them over the past four years and returned to their native Italy. On her departure, old Mrs Togneri pressed on the reluctant sergeant the gift of a beautifully embroidered linen tablecloth, a family heirloom which was to have formed part of a possible future daughter-in-law's bottom drawer.

For the next five years, until her death, a monthly Mass was said at St Aloysius church on behalf of old Mrs Togneri for the good intentions of the non-churchgoing Sergeant McKenzie.

In 1969, the whole of the Northern Division was served by two solitary police cars, two well used and well maintained Triumph Dolomite saloons, both equipped with what then constituted the very latest in communication technology, a two-way radio. One name, Echo Four, sufficed for both vehicles, since only one of them at any given time was on duty, the other being kept in reserve for maintenance and servicing. The active car was on duty 24 hours a day, with two men allocated to it for each shift, the driver and one other.

Any call received at Maitland Street which needed the presence of the car would be radioed to it, and any urgent call requiring immediate attention was prefaced by the words 'Code 21 Red'. On hearing this code the driver would ignore all else and drive with all speed to the scene of the emergency.

One particularly cold afternoon in November the car was being driven by one of Glasgow's most experienced and long serving drivers, 'Pedro' by nickname. His neighbour of long-standing was a constable who had just received the news of his promotion to the rank of sergeant, as a result of which this was to have been his last shift with Pedro on Echo Four. As a congratulatory gift he had been presented with a bottle of the best Chivas Regal by his driver, and this had been stowed away in the boot for consumption at some propitious moment. As they belted themselves into the car with the newly obligatory seat belts, the radio came to life.

'Code 21 Red! Code 21 Red! Proceed at once to the suspension bridge at Clyde Street. Two men in water, repeat, suspension bridge at Clyde Street. Two men in water'.

In just a few moments, despite the heavy traffic, Echo Four arrived at the scene of the accident and the two officers quickly took stock of the situation.

Two fully clothed men were struggling in the water at the far side of the river, watched silently by a small group of onlookers. Pedro and his companion were informed that one of the men was trying to commit suicide, and that the second man had jumped into the river in an attempt to save him. The current in the Clyde is quite strong at that point, and the two struggling men had been carried by it to the Carlton Place side of the river, where they could not be helped by the newly arrived constables. The two jumped into the car, sped back and over the Stockwell bridge, pulled up near the floating men, and dived into the icy waters in time to see one of them, the suicide, vanish under the murky surface. Fighting against the current, they grabbed hold of the survivor and with some effort, for the man was heavy and his clothes sodden with water, pulled him to the safety of the bank. The would-be rescuer, who was aged around 40, was in a poor state. The ten minutes immersed in the cold water and the struggle with the suicide had worn him out completely and he was shaking with a combination of exhaustion and cold.

Drastic measures were called for, so out came the bottle of Chivas Regal from the boot, from which he was given a more than generous tot in an attempt to heat and revive him. Other policemen had now arrived on the scene, and they began to pull out the dead body which had become snagged at the riverside. Echo Four drove the exhausted hero to his flat in the West End, where he immediately changed into warm, dry clothes and was given another tot of whisky. He was profuse in his thanks to the two constables, who also returned immediately to base to be dried out. Their prompt action in attempting to pull the two men from the river was noted and put them in line for a commendation from the chief constable, who was at that time David McNee. A commendation from the chief was not a novelty to the two, who were in possession of nearly a score each. Not because they were any braver than any other constable, but simply because as the crew of a police car they were called to dozens of emergency calls where the man on a beat would only occasionally come across one.

So they duly presented themselves for another award,

expecting the same old routine, but in addition to the commendations they were in for a rude surprise. The chief sat holding a letter. It was from the man they had pulled out of the river, asking for his thanks to be given to the two constables who had come to his assistance. It also commended the chief on the excellence of the whisky provided by the city for use in the first aid box of his patrol cars. It had come as a godsend to him after his immersion in cold water. The chief's comment to the two constables is not on record.

DNA and Bible John

Thirty-two years have gone by since the murder of a young woman after a night of dancing at the Barrowland ballroom in February 1968. Thousands upon thousands of words, factual and speculative, have been written since then about that murder and the murders of two other women in the following year in almost exactly the same circumstances. The three murders, in all probability committed by the same person, were never solved, and the mystery has gone down in the annals of criminal history as the case of Bible John. A book written in 1980, *Search for a Sadist* by the solicitor Charles Stoddart, based on first-hand material and on interviews with the leader of the last phase of the investigation, Detective Superintendent Joe Beattie, gives a factual and engrossing account of the crimes.

The unsolved Bible John murders became front-page news again in 1996 when it was decided to exhume the body of a man, John McInnes, who had been a suspect in the murders and who had been dead and buried for 16 years. Within the past few years technological advances in the forensic sciences have made possible the technique of DNA testing, whereby human tissue and fluids, no matter how small the sample, can be identified as belonging to a specific person. This is a powerful new tool in the field of criminal investigation, as important and far-reaching as was the development of fingerprinting at the beginning of the twentieth century, and it is now extensively made use of in the investigation of crimes.

A piece of clothing of one of the victims had been preserved by the police, with a stain on it which could possibly have been made by the murderer's body fluid. There is a similarity between the DNA pattern within the one family, and when this genetic DNA comparison technique became available, a brother and sister of McInnes agreed to have samples taken from them for analysis. Their genetic pattern was sufficiently close to that of the DNA on the clothing stain for a court order to be obtained for the exhumation of John McInnes' remains. The family layer was opened, the coffin of the mother, who had died after her son, was uplifted to give access to the coffin underneath and his remains removed for analysis.

Many misgivings were voiced about the practical, moral and ethical implications of the action. What could be usefully gained, apart from the demonstration of the powers of modern technology? If the procedure were to show that McInnes was indeed the guilty man, a dead murderer cannot be prosecuted, and if innocent, the process of exhumation and testing undoubtedly would rekindle interest and suspicion and would bring anguish to the surviving relatives of the exhumed man. The strength of all these arguments was increased tenfold by the fact that the dead man had been thoroughly investigated as a suspect at the time of the crimes, as were scores of others, and had been positively discounted as the possible murderer. Purely from a practical point of view the whole procedure was dismissed by many as being a waste of time and money and a publicity stunt to capture the headlines for those behind the project.

The matter had begun on the night of 22 February 1968 at the Barrowland ballroom in the Gallowgate near Glasgow Cross, a popular dance hall. A young nurse from the Victoria infirmary, Pat Docker, was a frequent visitor to the ballroom and was well known to the staff and the orchestra there. On the date in question she had spent the evening dancing with a variety of partners, then, after the last waltz, was seen to leave in the company of a young man. She lived with her parents in the Langside area near her place of work, and when she did not appear at home that night they were not unduly concerned, for it was not unusual for her to stay away all night during her time off. The following morning some boys playing in a lane near her house came upon the body of a naked woman lying half hidden in long grass and it did not take long for the police to establish that the body was that of Pat Docker. She had been stripped, raped and strangled with her own tights, and all her clothes and her handbag were missing.

A wide-ranging investigation was immediately launched. Her activities of the previous night were examined and the members of staff at the ballroom were closely questioned, as were many of the dancers there who had come forward at the request of the police. She had been seen by and danced with many during the course of the night, but no one could give a description of the man she had been seen leaving with after the last dance. Reports were made of her having visited the Majestic ballroom at the top of Hope Street that same night and the same procedure was gone through there. The investigation lasted for months without success, and the murder was left unsolved.

Then, in August of the following year, Jemima Mcdonald, a single mother with three children and, like Pat Docker, a well-known habitué of the Barrowland, failed to return home from a night's dancing. Her body was found on some waste ground not far from the house she shared with her sister. She too had been raped and strangled with her own tights, and her handbag was missing. Other similarities to the Docker murder was the fact that they were both brunettes and that they were both menstruating.

This time, however, the team of detectives on the case had better luck with their investigation, which followed the same pattern as that of Pat Docker. Their questioning gained them a good description of the man she had danced with most of the night and with whom she had been seen leaving. From this description, and for the first time in Scotland, an Identikit photo was assembled. It showed a man in his late twenties, with a clean, well shaven face, dark eyes and short reddish hair. He was described as being well dressed and about six feet in height.

The Identikit photo was circulated to the national press and was given to each member of the staff at the Barrowland. The police were not yet 100 per cent sure that the second crime had been committed by the murderer of Pat Docker. Both victims had danced at the Barrowland on the night of their murder, both had been raped and strangled, handbags were missing in both cases, both were brunettes, both were menstruating. All this could possibly have been coincidence, but then the matter seemed to have been resolved beyond question. Just two months after the murder of Jemima Mcdonald another woman was killed in exactly the same circumstances and, as far as the press was concerned, all doubt was removed.

Mrs Helen Puttock, the wife of a soldier, was also a frequent dancer at the Barrowland. Although newspaper speculations that a murderer was on the loose in the vicinity of the ballroom had frightened many dancers away, especially single females, Helen had carried on with her visits there. Moreover, on that night she felt particularly safe, for she was accompanied by her sister, Mrs Jeannie Williams. Helen was singled out for dance after dance by a presentable young man who had introduced himself as 'John'. In the course of the evening he had been introduced to the sister, Jeannie, who spent some time with him and her sister Helen, and the three of them left in the same taxi round about midnight. In the ballroom he had chatted incessantly about himself to the two women, and had represented himself as being intensely religious and quoted extensively from the Bible. Jeannie Williams was dropped off near her home in Scotstoun, and the taxi carried on with its two passengers towards Helen's home, a short distance away. The taxi dropped the two of them off about 50 yards from her house, and that was the last time she was seen alive. Her body was found early next morning by a woman emptying her rubbish in a back court a short distance from Helen's home. She had been raped, strangled with her own tights, her handbag was missing and she too was menstruating.

There seemed now, again as far as the press was concerned, not the slightest doubt about it, the search was on for a serial killer, and the case was now put in the hands of Detective Superintendent Joe Beattie. But this time there was a mass of information on which the investigation could be based. Jeannie, the sister, was, in the words of one of the detectives concerned in the case, 'a sharp wee woman' and acutely observant. As a result of her detailed description of 'John', which was corroborated by the taxi driver who had driven the two women, an accurate and detailed description of the wanted man was issued, and gave rise to what was probably the most concentrated manhunt in the history of the Scottish police. Because of the biblical quotations used frequently in his conversations with the two sisters in the ballroom and in the taxi the press called it 'The Hunt for Bible John'.

This time, instead of an Identikit picture of the man, so detailed was Jean's description of the murderer that an artist, Lennox Paterson of the Glasgow School of Art, was hired to paint a picture of him, and the finished article bore a very close resemblance to the Identikit which had been widely circulated at the time of the previous killing. One inexplicable feature of the case was the fact that the six stewards on duty that night at the ballroom, all of whom had been issued with the Identikit photo, failed to pick out Helen's companion that night as being the man the police were seeking to question

More than 100 men were assigned to the case in the Glasgow area, and police authorities throughout the country gave their co-operation. Completely new ground was broken in investigative techniques. A half-hour programme on the case was broadcast on TV, with a reconstruction of the crime played by actors and the help of viewers sought in the identification of the Identikit picture. This was the first time such a procedure had been carried out in Scotland. The help of a Dutch clairvoyant, Gerard Croiset, who had had some startling results when commissioned by the Dutch police in the investigation of murders, was sought. Thousands of door-to-door enquiries were made and scores of line-ups of people resembling the description of Bible John were attended by Jeannie Williams, the only person who could identify the killer and who had spent time in his company. Copies of the Bible John painting were sent to military centres throughout Britain and a Bible John HQ was set up at the Marine police station, which was swamped by reported sightings of the hunted man. A young man, John McInnes, from Stonehouse, kept popping up at the line-ups of suspects attended by Jeannie, but each time she was adamant that he was not the murderer. His appearance more or less matched that of Bible John, but so did scores of others who occasionally danced at the Barrowland ballroom.

The factors that made him the focus of suspicion were that, firstly, he came from a strict Plymouth Brethren family, a sect who shape their lives to the letter of the Bible and secondly, that he was given to boasting in pubs about the number of times he had been put in identification parades sandwiched between others who resembled the photo of the wanted man.

He was interrogated many times by Joe Beattie, an experienced officer, reputed to be possessed with an uncanny instinct in smelling out guilt. The detective came to the conclusion that McInnes was, without doubt, not the wanted man. Jeannie Williams was present at several of these interrogations, the better to observe the man suspected of murdering her sister, but she was just as adamant that McInnes was not the man she and her sister had spent some hours with on the night of her sister's death. She was dedicated to finding the guilty man, and had there been the slightest possibility that McInnes was that person it would have been seized on by her. Yet she declared on more than one occasion that McInnes was definitely not the man. The investigation dragged on for nearly a year and then slackened its intensity. Police had other duties to attend to, other crimes to investigate, and the manpower that could be focused on this case, no matter how notorious, was and is limited. The case of Bible John was relegated to the ranks of unsolved crimes.

Until 1996, that is, when the powers that be, for whatever reason, decided to exhume the grave of the long dead John McInnes, even though McInnes had been exonerated at the time of the crime, both by the man in charge of the investigation and by the principal witness. His body was exhumed so that his remains could be subjected to DNA matching.

The samples taken from the exhumed body were submitted to Cambridge University and the Institute of Forensic Medicine in Berlin for analysis and comparison with the stain on Helen Puttock's dress. The reports of these two agencies were not forthcoming for some time and were never made public, but the police authorities finally announced to the press that the results of the tests were inconclusive, and that no inference could be made from them.

And so the case of Bible John murders remains unsolved. There are those who say that the three murders might not be connected, that the evidence linking them to the one man is tenuous and coincidental and that the 'Bible John' title was purely a media invention which caught the public imagination and boosted the sale of newspapers. One fact is certain however, the cases of the murders of Pat Docker, Jemima Mcdonald and Helen Puttock remain unsolved, and the case of Bible John, if there is a Bible John, seems destined to go down in history as another Jack the Ripper story.

Recollections

Shopkeepers and traders in the Cowcaddens area were often plagued by hooligans bent on extorting small sums of money from the owners. This was termed 'going about at the demand'. Although occasionally traders were pestered during the day, especially vulnerable were those premises which traded mainly late at night. The neds would enter, usually in twos or threes, and ask for a small contribution 'to help them out'. A ten shilling note or a pound would usually suffice, thus avoiding broken windows or a broken head or both, and although it may not sound a great deal, to the long-suffering shopkeeper who had to fork out several times in the course of a week, and possibly to several different gangs, the sums doled out to avoid trouble mounted up.

The beat men helped as much as they could if approached by the victim, warning off predators and sometimes running them in on a breach of the peace charge, but such a course of action would only invite retaliation in the form of shop windows being broken during the night or threats of bodily harm to the trader. Small chip shops and cafés were much more vulnerable than larger establishments or pubs. The latter, no matter how small, were usually staffed by two or more barmen who were usually able to deal with the hooligans.However, in the main, chip shops were usually operated by the owner, with perhaps one or two female assistants, and for the sake of a peaceful existence many of these would grudgingly pay up.

Mr Andretti was the owner of such a shop, a small carry-out chip shop in St Georges Road, which he ran with the help of a woman assistant. He was a smallish, placid man, and to avoid any trouble with the neds, paid out a steady stream of ten shilling notes to hooligans coming in 'at the demand'. Ten shillings may not sound much, but the fact that in those days a fish supper cost a shilling puts its value in perspective. One day he decided that enough was enough. He resolved to take a stand and the story is taken up by one of the policemen on the beat at the time:

Do you remember wee Andretti, the wee stout fella who stayed in a flat three up in Renfrew Street? He had a wee carry-out in St Georges Road? It was a busy wee shop, but he was plagued with neds who used to come in at the demand. St Georges Road wasn't the worst place in the world, but it was just off the Garscube Road and the neds from there used to walk up and down it at night. The Tallys who had shops in rough areas or close by used to have a hard time of it with them. They were like the Pakis now, they had to stand a lot of abuse, the only thing was they had no race relations people then and we were the only ones they could turn to for support.

We used to drop in to wee Andretti's every night and he never complained, but one day he gets fed up and tells us that he's getting pestered with two neds at the demand who're giving him a lot of abuse and who are taking stuff away without paying. I partnered big John —— at the time and he listened and said to the wee man: 'Don't give the bastards anything. Get hold of a club, and when they come in you show them the club and if they don't want to pay for anything or if they want some money at the demand you tell them to eff off or you'll bust their bloody head in. Buy yourself one of our whistles and if you get any trouble give us a toot and we'll sort them out.'

So Andretti went to Crockett's in the Cowcaddens to

127

buy a whistle, he got a club as well and kept it hidden down at the side of the counter. One night we're standing at the Cross and we hear a whistle blowing like mad and it was coming from Andretti's shop. We go in and the place was a bloody mess, broken glass everywhere and there was a funny smell of burning. So we asked what had happened. Andretti said:

'Well, they came in and asked for two fish suppers and when I asked them for the money they told me to eff off and they wouldn't pay, so I brought the club out like you told me and I showed it to them, and the two of them grabbed it with both hands; I think they were going to use it on me, the only thing was, it wasn't a club. It was a bloody iron bar, and I had kept an end of it in the fire, and the top of it was nearly red-hot and the two of them left their bloody skin on it, it stuck to their hands and they started screaming blue murder and ran away.'

So we went out and asked around and somebody told us they had gone home to get their hands fixed. We went up to the neds' house to arrest the two of them for a breach of the peace, and there they were with their hands stuck out in front of them swathed in bandages, no able to do anything, being looked after by their wives and they're calling wee Andretti for everything. We got them hauled up in front of the magistrate and they were fined two pounds each for a breach of the peace. The wives had to take the money out of their pockets, they couldnay use their hands for weeks. Well, once word got round what had happened that stopped the neds. They left him alone after that.

One can well imagine what the results of that incident

would have been today. Andretti would probably be in the dock for having used excessive force in his own defence and not the two hooligans for having menaced him in the first place. The magistrates then showed no sympathy at all for such ruffians. No comments were made if anyone used robust methods to defend themselves or their property.

Another constable on a Cowcaddens beat tells this story:

There was a fella called George who ran the San Remo chip shop in Parly Road, a real tough shop that was, as tough as the Savoy and every bit as busy. George didn't bother with a chuckerout like the Savoy did, he sorted out the neds himself. He was tough and strong, hard as nails he was, worked out with weights in McMillan's gym every day and he never ran away from a fight. The local neds knew what he could do and left him strictly alone. One night three stranger neds from the Garngad come in and say, 'Gie us three fish suppers, ya effing Tally bastard.' When they start like that you know they're out for trouble and are no gonny pay for anything they get and are gonny give you a hard time, so what does George do? He looks at them and disnay say a word. He picks up a wee saucepan, dips it into the hot fat and throws it in their faces and when they're running about daft like burnt chickens yelling and screaming he goes out and blows the whistle. Big Tam and myself are standing in West Nile Street and we hear the whistle go so we go along and run the three of them in for a breach. We had to take them to the hospital first to get fixed up. Their faces were in a real helluva mess, all blistered up and they were greeting like wains. They got fined two quid each the next morning. They never went back, that taught them.

George was maybe a wee bit too rough at times, and he nearly killed a ned once. This one comes in and starts effing and ceeing at one of the girls for something or other and George goes over and tells him to keep quiet. The bloke doesn't take a blind bit of notice and keeps on swearing at the lassie, worse than ever, so George tells him again to keep quiet. So this time he starts swearing at George and starts calling him a Tally this and that. George grabs him by the collar with one hand and twists as hard as he could. The guy turns blue in the face and collapses frothing at the mouth and lies there stiff as a board. George gets a real big fright, he thought the guy was dead and blows the whistle and when we get there we thought the guy was dead too, but just in case we call an ambulance and take the guy to the Royal and it turns out he's still alive, and he's let out the next day OK. The doctor said he was lucky, one more twist on the collar and he would have snuffed it. So we tell George that maybe he ought to take it a wee bit easier with the neds.

In the sixties and seventies a familiar sight to the queues waiting to get into the picture houses in Sauchiehall Street and Renfield Street was a blind and handless beggar who sat with his back to the wall with a pleading placard strung around his neck. The pitiful sight evoked much sympathy and many a sixpence would be deposited in the man's upturned cap. The crowds might not have been quite so sympathetic had the reason for the man's disability been known to them.

Tom Galloway had been a petty criminal who preyed on shopkeepers and prostitutes, demanding money for the privilege of not having him smash your windows during the night or of not having your face damaged with a knife or a razor. One shopkeeper finally had enough and complained to the beat man, who cornered Tom and gave him the shaking of his life and a good belting around the ears with the promise of more serious things to come if he did not mend his ways, or at least transfer his activities to another area.

Spitting rage and hatred at the effrontery of the shopkeeper in seeking help from the police, Tom worked out a plan of revenge. He got together the necessary materials, manufactured a crude bomb and in the middle of the night crept to the back window of the premises, smashed the glass and tossed the bomb through the broken glass. The missile struck an almost invisible protective mesh on the inside of the window and bounced back into Tom's face and exploded, tearing off his hands and depriving him of sight.

Not all offenders were violent. Many preferred a more subtle approach in their attempts to gain an easy living and shunned all forms of violence. Again we have the words of the constable involved:

> There was another fella lived in the Cowcaddens, Peter Smiley his name was, everybody used to call him Peter the Creep. He was about 30 years old and although he was a bit of a weed he dressed well and always looked very smart, always looked neat and sharp with a fancy crombie coat and a nice tailor-made suit. He'd never done an honest day's work in

his life but he always had money, but wherever he got the cash, doing this and that, he had never been caught at it and he had never done any time. He used to go round big Glasgow offices with some plausible excuse or other, the girls always let him in, he looked so respectable. He would take a chance and when he managed to gain access to a room, maybe it was open, he'd whip away anything at all that he could put in his pockets then creep off without attracting any attention – hence the name Peter the Creep. The whisper was out that he picked pockets in posh places like the Malmaison and the Berkeley, but nobody had ever caught him at anything. Anyhow, one day Peter the Creep was in that fancy gents tailor in Gordon Street, Hector Powe's, near Renfield Street, sizing the place up and he notices a man paying for some things he had bought out of a fat wallet. The guy picks up his parcel and goes out and Peter follows him across the road and into Forsyth's, the posh gent's shop across the road. The man starts looking at sports jackets and Peter kids on he's looking at things too, but all the time he's keeping his eye on the man with the fat wallet. The man takes his jacket off to try another one on, and when he gets back he finds his wallet's gone, Peter had nicked it. The man comes up to the Maitland Street office right away to report the theft and tells us what had happened. His name was Ross Bowie, the man who owned the posh Arcadia ballroom next to the Locarno in Sauchiehall Street. He's sure that the fella who had been in Hector Powe's and in Forsyth's with him was the one who had nicked his wallet. Bowie was a very observant guy and he gives us a great description of the man. Right away I turn to my neighbour and say 'right, that's Peter the Creep', and we go out to look for him. Peter had very regular habits and he only drank in two bars, one at the top of Renfield Street, The Atholl Arms and the other one The Loughswilly Bar, no one had ever known him to go anywhere else, so we go first to the Loughswilly and we hit pay dirt right away.

As we go in we see Peter vanish into the toilets, he had spotted us coming in. So we follow him right in to the bog and grab him and go through his pockets, but there's nothing on him apart from a few shillings and he's swearing on a stack of bibles and on his mother's grave that he's done nothing. Naturally we don't believe a word he's saying, so we start searching the toilets and finally we find Ross Bowie's wallet stuffed behind a cistern in one of the booths. Believe it or not, there was about £600 in money in it, a bloody fortune, nearly all in £20 notes, those big things as big as blankets you used to get from the British Linen Bank, with a piece of paper in between the notes with Bowie's name on it.

So we take Peter in and although the money had not actually been found in his possession his fingerprints were on the wallet so he couldn't deny that he had handled it. He kept swearing blind that he had found the wallet in the pub, but all the evidence put together was too strong and he got done for it and gets six months in the calaboose. So he does the six months in Barlinnie, that was the first time he had ever done time and he didn't like it at all and he comes out and he comes to see me and says:

'Right, that's me finished, I don't want any more of that, I'm gonny go straight, can you help to get me a street traders licence?'

I'll always try to help a guy to go straight if I can and Peter wasn't a bad ned, never used violence on anybody, and maybe he did want to go straight, so I put a wee word in here and there and after a while he gets a street trader's licence and with this he got hold of a camera and started taking people's photographs in the street at half-a-crown a time.

That was a great thing in those days, you'd be out with your bird or your wife and kids and a street photographer would take your picture and a half-crown from you and give you a ticket to pick up the snapshot. But what Peter did, half the time he would have no film in the camera and he'd just take the punter's half-crown, hoping that he couldn't be bothered to pick up the snap, which happened often, so Peter would get the half crown for nothing.

[This must have been quite a common practise among street photographers. In February 1950 a Mr McIver was fined £10 at the district court for such an offence.]

There was a photographic shop in Cambridge Street where you had to pick the snaps up, and if there was nothing there for you, Peter's excuse was that the photo had not come out and to keep the punter quiet another one would be taken on the spot. Then later, to attract more business, Peter got a partner who had a monkey, and the ploy was to give the monkey to the man or the woman or the kids to hold and take their picture with the monkey. It went over in a real big way, fathers and mothers and kids used to queue up in Renfield Street to get their pictures taken by Peter and his partner. There was no need to work a flanker with an empty camera on the punters, business was so good.

But then one day the monkey nipped one of the weans with his teeth, just a nick, didn't even draw blood, but they got a fright in case it happened again worse and they would get in trouble. So they took the monkey, gave it half a bottle of whisky and pulled all its front teeth out. I kid you not. When we heard about it we called the cruelty people and they questioned the two but naturally they denied it and we could not get any witnesses so we could do nothing about it. The man on the beat began giving Peter a hard time because of that, so Peter and his partner and the monkey moved on, to Manchester, I heard, and we never saw him in Glasgow again.

The same officer recalls:

I would say it was safer to walk the streets then than now. By and large the neds wouldn't bother a passer-by, they used to fight among themselves and with other neds. The big weapon amongst themselves was the razor, the most dangerous thing. But there was a judge, Lord Carmont, who cured them of that habit. Put the skids under them he did. Every time someone came up on a razor charge he would show no mercy. Swish, ten years. Swish, ten years. Swish, ten years. Ten years meant ten years then. None of this getting out after a few years when you tell a trick cyclist you're a reformed man. That stopped them using razors. The first man to get ten years for razor slashing was a ned called Collins. One night he slashed the assistant manager of the Locarno in Sauchiehall Street. Collins got done for it and came up before Carmont. He got ten years. And everyone else who came up with a razor charge, bang, ten years, bang, ten years, just like that. That stopped the neds with the razors. It used to be that up Lyon Street, up the Garscube Road, all the neds had the Mark of Zorro, slash, across the face, but Carmont stopped that. Mark you, some of the other weapons they used weren't much better, chains, clubs with spikes, spiked knuckle-dusters, bayonets, knives and things like that, they didn't do you any good either but at least they didn't slice you up and cut deep like a razor did.

Sillitoe had a great influence, but his heavy squad men were fading out by that time, gradually, and the backbone of the force then were the ex-servicemen, who were coming out of the army, fit as fiddles and hard as nails. Most of the men on the beat during the war were war reserves, older men and not particularly fit and sometimes the neds were too much for them. Everbody in our shift was an ex-serviceman and we gave the neds a real fright.

We had a terrible spate of robberies at the Art School up in Renfrew Street. I had just started in the CID at the time. Purses and money and things were being lifted from the cloakrooms. It was obviously an internal job, couldn't have been anything else, nobody from the outside could have access, so we set a trap. There was this stuff, I can't remember its name now, it's invisible, but it sticks to the fingers and comes up with infra red light. So we dust the purses and money and some stuff gets stolen. So we check everybody in every class, not a sniff. There were only three people we had missed, and we said, no, it couldn't be any of them, they were all decent respectable people but we checked them before the Art School closed for the day, and lo and behold it was one of them, a girl, a doctor's daughter from Helensburgh. The father came up to get her the next day and I felt heart sorry for him, crying he was, but she was quite brassy about it. I forget what she got.

A crime is much easier to solve if it takes place inside somewhere rather than out in the open. In the open there maybe a better chance of getting witnesses, but against that, in a murder case for example, all the evidence can be destroyed by wind and weather. When a murder happens inside there's no weather to destroy evidence, but there's not much chance of getting witnesses. I remember one of the first cases I had in the CID. A father and a daughter had been murdered in a flat out in Govan. They had been killed with a knife, and whoever did it must have gone berserk; you never saw so much blood in all your life, it was everywhere, walls, floors, ceilings, everywhere. The father especially had been knifed about a dozen times, one of the blows was so hard that his chest had been pushed in, almost as if the guy had jumped on him. The knife was lying on the floor, all covered in blood, so we checked it for fingerprints but it was clear. It looked as if the murderer had tried to wash the blood off before he left, because there were a lot of blood tidemarks in the sink and a sheet had been used to dry himself. We questioned everybody in the close but nobody knew anything and if they did they weren't saying. Now, when you get a murder like that you'll usually find that the murderer is someone the victim knows, somebody who has a grudge or hate against him. A burglar might knife you to get away, but he's not going to hang around and cut you up and mess you up like these two were. Now, the dead man had three more daughters who lived up the next close and a cousin lived there too, so we questioned the cousin but couldn't come up with anything. You can get a feeling about a guy, and I felt sure in my bones that he was the one who had done it, but what can you do without some evidence? The fingerprint boys were still working away in the house but nothing was coming up.

I started to nosey around the lobby; the floor was covered with linoleum and on it I could see funny looking red marks in among the pattern. So I called the print boys, and did they not turn out to be toe-prints! The murderer had taken his shoes and stockings off to wash himself and had walked out barefoot and left a toe-print. Now, a toe-print is just as good as a fingerprint, so we went back to the cousin and asked to take his toe-print and he broke down and confessed. Quite a unique case it was.

Misfits

Many a man has joined the force for lack of other available jobs, with no clear idea of what the job entails. Disenchantment can soon set in when the realities of policing are encountered. Some thole it out, take the line of least resistance and grab the first opportunity of retiring with a pension, others take a more positive line and cut the Gordian knot:

In 1952, at the age of 24, Neil Simpson had tried his hand at many occupations. He was good with his hands and instinctively seemed to know what was wrong with any piece of malfunctioning machinery and for a time found reasonable wages and job satisfaction as a mechanic in his home town of Perth. Good with his hands though he may have been, he was even better with his feet and could dribble a football with the best of them, putting this talent to use in the occasional football match with a local amateur team. He was six feet in height and strongly built and his skill and athleticism came to the attention of a talent scout from a well-known second division team. He was made an attractive offer, a year's contract at eight pounds per week and a five pounds bonus for each win.

This was far more than he could earn in the job he was doing at the time, so Neil accepted and embarked on what he hoped might be a quick run up the ladder of footballing success. Disaster struck during his third game as a professional. Emerging awkwardly out of a hard tackle, he felt a searing pain in his leg, was stretchered off and told after X-ray examinations the following day that the ligaments in his knee were badly torn and that he might never be able to play competitively again. The year's contract expired and was not taken up again by the club, so Neil began looking for employment and his attention was taken by a poster urging young men to take up a career in the Glasgow police.

Since he was as yet unmarried and had no ties in the Perth region, the thought of patrolling Sauchiehall Street and other famous city thoroughfares with their glittering shops, glamorous theatres and cinemas appealed to him and he duly presented himself at the recruiting office in Glasgow. The damage to his knee was no hindrance to him in passing the various physical tests he was subjected to, and soon he was in the Oxford Street training centre, learning the basic skills of the policeman. He was ready then to be assigned to an experienced neighbour, and was given a veteran of more than 20 years service who proceeded to indoctrinate him into the delights of patrolling out of St Rollox, a substation of the Northern Division, situated in the north-eastern part of the city. The area to be patrolled from there, which encompassed some of the most unappealing places to be found in a city in the throes of a massive redevelopment, stretched from Sighthill cemetery in the west to Blackhill in the east. Building sites proliferated, on all sides were disused workshops, litter-strewn streets and pavements and semi-derelict tenements, the few inhabitants of which did not take kindly to the sight of a police uniform. The dream of cinema palaces and well-lit, shop-lined streets with their glamorous theatre-goers evaporated. Neil takes up the tale:

> I'd never seen such a place. Bloody awful. If I'd known I might have ended up in a place like that I never would have joined the polis. Full of warehouses and vacant bits of ground and the odd tenement building in between, full of neds and their families. There were a lot of new houses going up for slum clearance schemes and the whole area looked like a dirty bombsite. The roads were terrible, all

pot-holes, the lighting was bad and on night shift you could swear there was someone waiting for you behind every corner. The people who lived there looked as if they had just come out of the Stone Age and there was nobody around to say a civil word to. My neighbour was an old hand and was used to it, but he got cheesed off too at times, and griped about the lucky so-and-sos who had the good beats around the middle of town and moaned on and on about favouritism and how he was just waiting for the pension to come along and so on and so forth. We had a great sergeant too. Big help he was. He never got his hands or feet dirty, couldn't get away from the place fast enough. There was a tram terminus next to the box. He'd wait for us to arrive and when we got there he'd say:

'Listen', and you could hear a rammy going on somewhere down in the tenements, shouts and yells and glass breaking and things like that.

'The natives are restless tonight,' he'd say. 'Get down there and sort them out. That's the last tram, I'm off,' and he'd bugger off and leave you.

To show you the kind of place it was and what kind of people lived there. One night somebody starts yelling like mad for the polis and we could hear a lot of noise coming from a social hall a bit away, sounded like a real big rammy was going on. So we go down to see what was up. There was a wedding party on, and they had been fighting all over the place. Wild it was, broken bottles everywhere, tables smashed, everybody roaring drunk. A big bloke comes over and we ask him what had started it. He says: 'It wuz a dead liberty, so it wuz. The best man wuz caught shaggin' the bride, and that wuz when the fight started.' So we look at one another and wonder what the hell to do. Just as we're standing another big guy comes out and waves his hands. 'S'aw rite, s'aw rite, nae mair bother. He's apologised to the groom!'

You wouldn't believe the types who lived there, some of them dragged their knuckles on the pavement when they walked. Well, one night after six weeks on the job I'm left there on my own. Somebody had called in sick and they were short-handed and couldn't give me a mate. There were a couple of bikes there that we used, the beat was so big you couldn't do it all on foot, so I get on one and start pedalling round the streets and lanes, getting more and more cheesed off by the minute. It was scary around there on your own, I tell you. All you had was your whistle, and who would hear it if you needed help? You could get your throat cut in the dark and nobody would find your body till the next day, if then. There was a big yard about half a mile from the box with two nightwatchmen in it, so I stop there for a while for a heat and a wee blether, and when I come out has somebody not stolen the bloody bike !

So I walk back to the box, really cheesed off now, and I sit there thinking about the bloody awful place I've landed myself in and is it going to be like this for the next 30 years, and I keep thinking about it until the first tram of the morning arrives. I jump on it, go back to my digs, phone them up at headquarters and leave word that I'm not going back. I sent back the uniform and never went near them again. I think they still owe me some money for the time I put in that week.

✳   ✳   ✳

Constable John Jackson had but two interests in life, strong drink and golf. He had very little interest in his chosen profession. He did not regard his job as a policeman as a way of serving the public and protecting property and being paid for those functions, as the bulk of other policemen did. To him it was merely a way of getting a weekly wage. There were perks in the form of a free and plentiful supply of whisky from indulgent publicans on his way around the beat, and it provided him with enough free time to play golf several times each week on the excellent corporation courses possessed by Glasgow in 1954. He was a golf fanatic, a fanaticism fueled by a week spent in Carnoustie a year before, watching Ben Hogan win the Open Championship. He himself was a reasonable golfer with a handicap of eight, and ever since that week spent in watching the golfing perfection of Ben Hogan, his ambition was to get hold of the best set of clubs he could and bring his handicap down as near scratch as possible. His set of clubs consisted of a fairly good matched set of Forgans worth about £30 or so and although he knew that good scoring in golf depended on the ability of the man and not so much on the design of the clubs, he ached to get his hands on a really top class brand of golfing equipment. But the matched sets bearing the names of Tommy Armour, Bobby Jones, Walter Hagen and Henry Cotton were well outside the reach of his ten pounds a week salary.

It is perhaps difficult to appreciate the temptations confronting the likes of a policeman in the course of his duties on a city centre beat 50 years ago. Paid a pittance to protect goods and property which he himself could never hope to acquire, it is a tribute to the integrity and honesty of the police that so very, very few succumbed in any way to the temptations that surrounded them.

For these temptations were many. The 20 quid or so from a bookie for information of an impending raid. The occasional fiver from a shopkeeper for a blind eye turned to a minor transgression of a local by-law. The quick tenner from someone in the food trade known to have dealings with black market goods. The friendly gifts from pawnbrokers whose stocks were not too carefully scrutinised. The backhander from a shebeen gone unreported, the bung from a pub for turning a blind eye to an infringement of the licensing laws, the list of temptations could go on and on. The conditions that made these inducements tempting are gone, and the salary of a police officer now is such that things they are called upon to protect could be within their reach, even the modern equivalent of a 1954, £200 set of Ben Hogan golf clubs.

That year John was assigned the number six beat in the Cowcaddens, which ran east from Hope Street and along the northern pavement of Sauchiehall Sreet. Lumley's, one of the most famous sports outfitters in Glasgow, has its premises there, next to Lauders pub. John passed it every day in the course of his duties, and one day he stopped, hypnotised by the window display.

There, prominently displayed at the price of £200, was a magnificent set of matched Ben Hogans, housed in a handsome leather bag. Day after day as he passed he looked and looked and his desire grew. Two hundred pounds for a set of golf clubs was completely out of the question on his salary.

The allocation of the number six beat had been a real bonus for him. The beat contained some of the best pubs in town and the supply of whisky from them was unlimited, so much so that he began to take the odd drink or so whilst still on duty, something which even the heaviest drinkers in the force did not do, their tipple was always restricted to off-duty hours. Tormented by the daily sight of the Ben Hogan clubs, and in the midst of the slight alcoholic haze that now accompanied his every action, a plan of action was evolved. His night shift period arrived, and on the first suitable occasion, in the middle of the night, when the streets were completely deserted, he heaved a large brick through Lumley's plate glass window and took possession of the set of Ben Hogans.

He hid them in a nearby safe place, then proceeded to the Hope Street box to phone in his discovery of the broken window. Hurry Bros were called out, the window was replaced and the robbery noted and investigated by the CID and put down as the depredation of passing hooligans. Allowing a reasonable time to pass, John began using the clubs on his regular outings to the corporation courses, but despite the constant drinking his brain still functioned well enough to have him discard the handsome leather bag which would undoubtedly have attracted attention and use his own plain canvas one to carry the stolen clubs. A long period went by, during which John, by now probably classifiable as an alcoholic, might well have ceased to remember the origin of his clubs, and the time for the yearly police golf matches arrived. These matches were played on Cawder golf course in Bishopbriggs, and in his first match John was drawn with a sergeant in the CID. During the course of the game the sergeant became interested in John's Ben Hogans, examined them, remembered the Lumley's robbery, investigated further and that was that. John was charged with theft, tried and convicted and sentenced to six months in prison. Nothing is known of his fate after his release.

The Heroes

The definition of the word 'hero' is given in the *Oxford Dictionary* as 'one who is distinguished by exceptional courage and fortitude'. By that definition, a very large percentage of the men who walked a beat in Glasgow since the police force began could be classified as heroes. In the police, as in the armed forces, some men are singled out for special mention because of some outstanding act which has required bravery and a disregard for personal safety far elevated above the normal dictates of duty. The following are cases where the policeman was chosen for special commendation:

In a city that had much more than its fair share of violent and lawless districts, Blackhill in Glasgow was high on the list of undesirable places to patrol as a policeman. Built as a housing scheme for the rehousing of some of the inhabitants of slum areas that were in the process of being demolished, in a short space of time Blackhill had become every bit as bad, if not worse, than the slums it was meant to replace. The corporation policy was to rehouse the more respectable slum dwellers in the high amenity housing estates and the problem families together elsewhere, thus creating high unemployment and high crime areas. Blackhill was one such area. Housebreaking and vandalism was rife, houses built as substitutes for the foul slums were as bad as the houses they were meant to replace. Problem families from the Gorbals and the Saracen areas had been decanted there and had brought their way of life with them, making Blackhill a depressing crime- and vandal-ridden zone that was to be avoided. Unemployment and life on the 'Broo' was the norm. Bands of youths slouched at street corners with nothing to do but smoke Woodbines, drink cheap wine and plan for the next act of vandalism and theft. Blackhill was not far from being a no-go area for the police, who had to patrol in twos. Should they have had occasion to arrest someone, it was likely that a hostile crowd would gather, shouting threats and obscenities until the Black Maria left with its cargo. Fortunately, by then, a two-way radio system was used by the Glasgow police which meant that back-up could quickly be summoned.

One night in the spring of 1966 Constables Tom Baird and Willie Graham were on their way to do a tour of duty in guarding a block of four shops in the centre of Blackhill which were regularly being broken into, despite a array of steel bars and metal doors built into the premises as protection. Each night four policemen were assigned to watch over the block, in the hope of arresting the thieves. On the way there they saw two men attempting to force open the door of a pub, the Rob Roy Bar, and immediately challenged them. The reply was a blast from a sawn-off shotgun. Although fired at fairly close range, by a miracle the shot missed, giving the two men time to dive for cover behind some dirt bins as the gunman let loose with another barrel, which also missed its intended target. As the gunman was reloading, the two constables made a charge at him, but not before two more shots were fired at them, one of which wounded Tom Baird in the head. They finally came to grips with the man and disarmed and arrested him. For this they were awarded the George Medal.

In the summer of 1954 Constable Tom McShane was walking along Craigendmuir Street in the Blackhill, on his way to join his beat partner for the beginning of the late shift. A few yards ahead of him a man came out of a shop, holding a revolver in his hand. McShane stopped dead in his tracks, and as he did so the man aimed the gun at him and fired. The distance was no more than 20 feet or so, and yet the shot missed. McShane crouched and ran hard at the gunman, knocking him to the ground and wrenching the gun from his hand. A fierce struggle ensued and after a few moments McShane was able to subdue and handcuff the gunman. However, a second problem had arisen for the constable. A hostile crowd had gathered, shouting abuse at the beleaguered policeman, who had no means of calling for help. But aid came from an unexpected source. In Craigendmuir Street there was a block of houses used by the Glasgow corporation as a refuge for destitute, unmarried mothers. The needs of these poor unfortunate women were seen to by two agencies, a nursing association known as 'The Green Ladies', who visited the sick and needy in the area, and an order of nuns from a Glasgow convent. The Green Ladies were based outside the housing estate and were equipped with distinctive green painted cars, which enabled them to visit and give help where required.

The nuns, who took care of unmarried mothers, lived on the estate and had a house in Craigendmuir Street directly opposite the refuge. Two nuns were on duty in the house that day, and they watched horror-stricken at the drama unfolding just a few yards away. There were two categories of person who could walk the streets of those lawless slum clearance areas with impunity then, without fear of molestation or attack. Doctors and their nurses and any priest or minister of religion could go about their business with impunity, for even in the criminal mind certain actions were beyond the pale. The green ladies could leave their cars unattended as they took care of their patients, in the knowledge that no one would steal or damage them, and no one would dare touch a nun. Immunity from attack in such areas no longer exists for anyone now. There are places in Glasgow where a doctor will not visit at night without a police escort.

The two nuns saw the hostile crowd gather and, realising the policeman's danger, ran out, faced down the yelling mob, escorted him and his prisoner into the sanctuary of their house and phoned for help. Dozens of police were soon on the scene in Black Marias, forcing their way through the several hundred strong crowd and Tom McShane and his prisoner were led away to safety through the milling abuse-chanting mob.

Tom McShane was awarded the BEM (British Empire Medal) for his bravery and the nuns were left alone to get on with their work.

✳   ✳   ✳

In 1952 the Hyndland district of Glasgow was a genteel place in which to live. The tenements were red sandstone with tiled closes, the so-called 'wally close', with stairways that boasted heavy banisters of the best mahogany. The back yards had neatly tended lawns, the flats were spacious, and the tenants of these houses were seen as the peak of respectability. The district formed part of the west end and therefore had remained free of the slums that had grown up round other parts of the city. The tenants of these flats would probably have been categorised as being of the lower middle class and the beat was regarded as being a very cushy one by the men assigned to patrol it. There were few shops in the area, mainly at the top end of Clarence Drive, which meant that there were not many premises to check during a night shift, but by the same token there were not many places you could visit to while the time away. The occasional hooligan did trickle up from Partick via Gardner Street, but since the pubs in the Hyndland area were well run places where such people were immediately shown the door, there was nothing to encourage them to dally there. Although the closes were open to the pavement, since the need for security doors had not developed yet, the iron gates leading to the backyards were always kept locked at night, thus depriving any would-be burglar of their favourite means of access for a housebreaking spree.

Constable John McLeod had just come on duty for the night shift and as a precursor to another boring night on this tranquil beat, had begun his tour of inspection of shop premises. Some distance away he noticed a young man slouched up against a close entrance. He stood slumped against the railings, hands in pockets, and as McLeod approached the youth, who could have been no more than 16 or 17 years old, he was suddenly confronted by a pistol aimed straight at his head. Before he could utter a word the youth had pulled the trigger and the bullet grazed the officer's temple. McLeod grappled with his attacker, and despite his wound, which was streaming blood, he kept the would-be killer in a firm grip.

A policeman coming in the opposite direction, from Great Western Road, had heard the shot, and as he ran towards the scene, McLeod, by now weakened by loss of blood, was forced to release his prisoner. The gun had fallen to the ground in the struggle, the boy rushed to pick it up, and cold-bloodedly shot McLeod in the head. The constable died instantly. The gunman then aimed a shot at the advancing policeman, who fell with a shattered kneecap. Without a single word the boy then placed the muzzle of the gun against his own temple and shot himself dead. It was a senseless crime, motivated by what? Drugs? Drink? Insanity?

John McLeod was posthumously awarded the BEM.

In 1952 Constable Andrew Cruickshank, on night shift duty in Lambhill Street in Govan, became aware of a curious creaking noise coming from a tenement. As he came closer to the source of the noise a piece of falling masonry shattered on the pavement in front of him. The creaking noise became louder, smaller pieces of masonry began to fall, and he suddenly realised that the tenement was beginning to collapse. He rushed into the first close and ran up the stairs banging at doors as he went, alternately shouting and blowing his whistle. He repeated the procedure in the three closes of the tenement, kicking and banging at doors as hard as he could, then herded the bewildered and sleep-dazed occupants into the safety of the street. He then entered every single house, a total of 36 in all, to make sure that all the occupants had left for safety. During all this, more and more bits of the tenement were falling off, and finally, about ten minutes after the constable was satisfied that no one was left in the building, the entire structure collapsed in a cloud of masonry, splintered wooden rafters, bricks and dust. One shudders to think what fate would have befallen the residents had it not been for the young officer's bravery and presence of mind.

Constable Cruickshanks was awarded the BEM.

The Women

Even in the days when the sight of a woman in police uniform was unheard of and the idea of serving policewomen unthought of, women played a very significant part in the policing of the Glasgow streets. Their service and dedication was in their roles as the wives of the men who patrolled the beat, for they shared vicariously in the dangers faced by their menfolk and their lives were fraught by worry and concern as their husbands faced the dangers inherent in a policeman's life. Mention has to be made of the stresses and strains that a policeman's duties imposed on wives and on marriages. Many an anxious wife would await with taut nerves the return of her husband from a night shift in a bad area, and many were the occasions when bruises and contusions sustained in a brawl or in an arrest were attended to by a concerned wife. There were other pressures too. Social contacts were in some cases limited to other police families, something that was encouraged by the provision of 'police houses' for the exclusive use of married officers. A policeman tended to feel himself ever so slightly apart from his neighbours in society, who were never fully at their ease with him. As one long-retired policeman puts it:

> It didn't pay to get too pally with your neighbours. You never knew when you were going to have to tick one off for something as part of your duty, or maybe even arrest him, so you tended to keep yourself a wee bit standoffish. I sometimes thought they were a wee bit careful about what they said or talked about in your company, they never let their hair down 100

per cent with you, just in case they let something slip out that might give away something about themselves or somebody else.

A Policeman's address was never given out readily. They never knew if it might fall into the hands of some hooligan or convicted criminal seeking revenge, and phone numbers were jealously guarded. It was impossible, however, to keep the nature of the job secret. Nowadays a policeman leaves his home dressed in civvies and changes into uniform at his station. No one need know what his job is. Then, a policeman had to change in and out of uniform at home. His occupation was obvious as soon as he crossed his threshold. Policemen's children very often suffered from the vengeful jeers and taunts of their school mates, for in some districts there was sure to be a school where one or more of the parents had been put behind bars by a policeman father.

There is one case of a constable who lived in Dobbie's Loan and who had occasion to arrest two safe-blowers who subsequently were given a stiff jail sentence. Their respective offspring all attended the same school and because of threats against them, the policeman's children had to be escorted to school and back home each day. After some time the mother could no longer stand the strain and her husband had no option but to resign from the force and seek work elsewhere for the sake of his family. Such a scenario was repeated with variations in many a school playground and many a good policeman has left the force to seek other employment because of such domestic constraints and pressures.

Sometimes the solution to a problem of that nature was found by the policeman concerned, as a constable recalls:

I used to have a neighbour on the beat in the Cowcaddens. He was a good cop who stood no nonsense from the neds and ran a peaceful beat. Some ned must have had it in for him for some reason or other. He had a phone in the house and his wife kept getting threatening calls, saying what was going to happen to her husband, he was going to get done, he was going to get slashed, she'd never see him alive again, and so forth. It wasn't easy to trace calls then, it took a lot of time and sometimes the ned on the phone would talk dirty to the woman and we had no idea who it was. She had got to be a bag of nerves and couldn't stand it any more, so my mate was seriously thinking of packing it in for her sake. They got the phone number changed and the ned couldn't make calls to her any more.

But one day a bloke follows her down into the Cowcaddens subway and starts talking dirty to her and tells her about the bad things that are going to happen to her husband, and she realises it was the same man who had been making the phone calls. She runs away without getting a good look at him, the Cowcaddens subway then had a very badly lit entrance, but even in the poor light she had noted one thing, he had no pinkie on one hand. At that we knew right away who the ned was! He was a real evil bastard, a pimp we had done dozens of times for assaults on women and thieving and things and this must have been his way of trying to get his own back. So the next night we went up to the Round Toll bar, we were off duty and we had civvies on, we knew he always drank there and we waited for him coming out. It was no use bringing him in and charging him. It was a hard thing to prove and a good brief could have got him away with it no bother. So we sorted him out, I tell you. We grabbed him and pulled him into the backyard. There wasn't an inch of him we didn't do over. We left him there with a broken arm, some cracked ribs and a busted head and then phoned an ambulance. He was three weeks in the hospital. We told him that if he breathed a word about it or if he ever molested anybody again he would be back in there permanently. That cured him, he never did another assault on women or bother anybody after that.

It is highly probable that nothing much may have changed as far as the strain on the policeman's wife goes, but as far as women's position in the force is concerned, an enormous change has taken place. The need for women in some aspects of policing had long been realised by the more progressive elements in a male-dominated establishment. A woman who has been sexually assaulted or a child who has been abused will speak more readily to a woman than to a man. By 1920 Glasgow had 11 women in the force who dealt with such cases.

The number of women in the force increased very slowly, for the Scottish Police Federation on the whole was not in favour of the use of women in the police. Moreover, service in the force, limited as it was, had no attraction for women. The pay was poor, less than half that of a man and their authority, with no power of arrest, was very limited. But in the early thirties the far-seeing Percy Sillitoe saw the need to have the number of women in the force expanded and sought to encourage recruitment by offering better pay and a greater variety of duties. Women were given the title of police auxiliaries and were trained in the Scottish training school for policewomen in Newton Place. The minimum height was set at five foot four inches, only unmarried females were considered and they had to resign from the force if they did marry. At the beginning of World War II the recruitment campaign for special constables to replace the men who had gone to active service was extended to women and the Women's Auxiliaries became known as the Women's Police Corps. Their duties and powers were increased as well. Many Black Marias were now driven by women and all members of the Women's Corps were given powers of arrest.

However, their duties in the main still consisted of taking and copying statements from witnesses, the questioning of women and children victims of sexual abuse and the cataloguing of items of evidence. The larger police stations had female turnkeys who searched and attended to female prisoners. It was not until the mid-fifties that women were introduced to other aspects of police work. They were assigned work on school crossings and supervised the use of the newly introduced zebra pedestrian crossings. In the sixties a policewoman's pay began to approach that of a policeman, and slowly the status of the policewoman grew until finally, in 1975, having achieved full equality with men, policewomen were assigned shift duties side by side male officers.

In the police force of today, of the 7,200 serving officers in the Strathclyde region, 1,126 are women. These policewomen have the same status as their men colleagues, face the same dangers, have the same career opportunities, and share identical remuneration.

Equality for women in the police was slow in coming, took the best part of half a century to achieve and mirrored the changing role of women in society. The slowness of change as far as active policing is concerned is understandable. Police work is not all that different from soldiering. In the twentieth century there has always been a place in the armed forces for women in ancillary posts such as nursing, driving, secretarial and organisational roles, but these were merely extensions of work already done by women in civilian life.

Fifty years ago it would never have been expected that a woman should face up to the prospect of a night shift alone on the Garscube Road or the Garngad with the dangers lurking there in dark and dismal backyards and in dimly lit closes. It would never have been expected that a woman should be thrown into the middle of a gang fight in the Gorbals, would have helped to break up a riot at a football match, restored order in a pub brawl, or have handled a 'Belfast Boat' situation.

But the nature of policing has changed as have technology and the environment. Conditions of service are not the same. There is no cold, wet and windy beat to trudge around now, the warm Panda car has taken the drudgery and misery out of that. There is no Acme Thunderer to blow in the hope that a colleague will hear it and come to assist in a crisis situation, the two-way radio and the mobile phone have seen to that. The danger is still there, even greater, given the growing violence in society and the constraints the police must operate under, but constant contact is now maintained between the police and their headquarters, and if assistance is required it can arrive in moments in the form of a fast van or police car.

The first women with full equality with their male partners first appeared on the beat in 1973. This move was greeted with scepticism and hostility by the older constables. A veteran constable who in his last few months of service was assigned a woman as partner recalls:

> Women were getting put out on beats together with men and I was given this wee lassie to work with. I didn't fancy it one bit. The beat's no place for a woman I thought, and worse still, the super says to me 'keep your eye on her'. How can you? If you get in a rammy it takes all your time to look after

yourself, let alone a woman and you like to have a neighbour by you that can pull his weight, not one that you have to look after. So I start laying it off to the super and he gives me a right bollocking and tells me I've been given an order and that's enough. Well, without me knowing it, all this time the wee lassie that's been assigned to me is standing behind the door and hears every word I've said. I was sorry she'd heard what I said, so I say to her, 'look, it's nothing personal, but you don't know what it can be like out there, it's you I'm thinking about if those neds really get rough. Anyhow, if we get in a rammy put your back up against a wall and don't move from there, I'll handle anything that happens, just make sure you don't get yourself hurt.'

One night we had to go on duty at the Locarno in Sauchiehall Street to help control the crowd. There was a group called Deep Purple on and hundreds of fans couldn't get in, the place was packed to overflowing, and the ones outside began to get nasty and started milling around and dunting cars and shouting and swearing and throwing bottles and stuff like that. We go in to break things up and I get rough with one or two of the neds and out of the corner of my eye I can see that when the lassie, Jean, I think her name was, gets in amongst them they seem to jump back from her as though they had been stung or something. Anyhow, that finishes up OK and we get the crowd dispersed and then we're told to go to the Green's Playhouse along the road where there's a bit of a rammy going on. Another pop group, I forget their name, were appearing at the ballroom, and what had happened was, the stewards had been taking a bung and letting a lot of people without tickets in at the side door, and the place was packed already and the ones with tickets couldn't get in. They were naturally worked up about it, a lot of them had been drinking and the screw-tops were beginning to fly. Some more cops had arrived, so we go in again to disperse the crowd and the same thing happens, neds are jumping away from Jean as though they had got an electric shock or something. One of them comes running over to me and says, 'See that bird in the uniform over there, she gave me a jag with something.'

I tell him to eff off, but after everything's quietened down I ask Jean what the ned was talking about. Well, she had cut about two inches off a hatpin and had stuck it into a wee rubber ball and she held the ball in her fist with a bit of the point sticking up between her fingers and everytime a ned came near her she gave him a good jag with it. Maybe she wasn't supposed to do anything like that, but it certainly kept the neds away from her and it made me realise she was capable of taking care of herself. I didn't worry about her after that.

There is no record of such an item of self-defence having become standard equipment for police!

In September 1972 a policeman on the Victoria bridge saw a woman clamber over the parapet and make her way down to an outside ledge. The woman was distraught and paid no heed to the attempts of the constable to persuade her back on to the pavement. He summoned help, and among the officers who arrived on the scene was a woman constable, Vivian Tweedie.

Despite the dreadful weather, with a driving rain making it difficult to maintain a foothold, Constable Tweedie slowly made her way down to the ledge beside the woman and eventually persuaded her to return to safety. Because of the overhang of the bridge this proved exceptionally difficult and dangerous, and the constable had to await the arrival of the fire brigade before she and the woman could be hoisted to the street and safety.

Vivian Tweedie was awarded the Queen's commendation for brave conduct for her action. At that time there were only 101 women serving in the force.

These days, women throughout the UK are accepted, both by the population and by their male colleagues, as a full and integral part of the police, and their contribution to the maintenance of law and order and the investigation of crime has been invaluable. The ladder of advancement is open to them, and although as yet very few of the higher posts are occupied by women, the way forward does not rule out the emergence of women in the highest echelons of the force. Public acceptance of such a situation is made easier by the power and influence of the media, where programmes depicting police work, such as the popular and long-running *The Bill* regularly feature women in some leading roles.

Disasters

The occupation of the fireman is fraught with environmental dangers and the history of the fire brigade is punctuated by the names of the many firemen who have been killed in the course of their duties. To a certain degree the police share these dangers, for where there is a fire there are also police and although they may not be actively engaged in fighting a blaze, they operate in close proximity to the firefighter, and to that extent share in the dangers that confront them. Incredible as the statistic may seem, in the year 1961, the last for which this statistic is available, the police attended 4,017 fires in the Glasgow area. Although the bulk of these may have been simple chimney fires, a common occurrence in the days of the coal-burning tenement grate, or backyard midden fires caused by the smouldering ashes sometimes dumped there, many of them must have been major conflagrations involving danger to life.

Ever since the disastrous Star Cinema fire of 1884 in Partick, in which 14 children died, crushed and asphyxiated in an attempt to escape the burning building, the presence and efforts of the police at such disasters is well catalogued. At that fire alone dozens of firemen and policemen were treated for burns and smoke inhalation in their efforts to free the children, and had it not been for their intervention, the death toll would have been much higher. More recently there are many instances of police bravery at the scene of fires. In May 1949, Grafton's gown shop in Argyle Street was the scene of a dreadful fire. In it 13 shop assistants died, unable to escape from the building because of inadequate fire escape facilities. Ten policemen had to be treated at the Royal Infirmary for serious burns and smoke inhalation injuries sustained in their efforts to free the trapped girls.

In the early sixties a paint factory went ablaze in Dobbies Loan. The area at that time was a hotch-potch of factories, small workshops and scores of sub-standard tenements. Thousands of gallons of paint and flammable material burned, giving out dense clouds of noxious gases. Many firemen and police were overcome by fumes, and several officers were given commendations for their efforts in helping the tenants of nearby tenements to safety.

In November 1968 a fire started in an upholstery factory in James Watt Street. The blaze spread rapidly throughout the three floors of the building, trapping 22 workers behind iron-barred windows. The fire escape doors at the back were blocked, and despite all the efforts of firemen and police the 22 trapped men and women died. Here again several police officers suffered injuries in their efforts to help the trapped workers and had to receive hospital treatment. In addition to injuries caused by smoke inhalation, many had severe hand burns caused in attempts to force open the bars of the blocked windows.

In 1971 Constable John McPhee was commended by the Secretary of State for Scotland for his bravery in attempting to reach a fire on the eighth floor of a building, and in the same incident Constable David Peterson died from inhalation of smoke as he was trying to effect a rescue. The Secretary of State's commendation in his case was awarded posthumously.

These are but a few of the thousands of occasions where the men on the beat have risked their health and lives in the course of duty.

Perhaps the two most written about Glasgow disasters of recent times have been the Cheapside fire and the Ibrox stadium disaster.

At ten minutes past seven on the night of the 29 March 1960, the manager of the Eldorado ice-cream factory in

Cheapside Street was paying a routine visit to his premises. Next door to the factory stood a bonded warehouse, consisting of a large six storey building with basement. As he passed by it he noticed a strong smell of burning and on looking up he could see smoke coming from a second floor window. He immediately dialed 999 for fire and police. About five minutes later police appeared on the scene and, exactly nine minutes after the alarm had been given the first fire appliances arrived. By this time smoke was billowing from the building and, as the extent of the fire was realised, more appliances were radioed for by the fire officer in charge.

More police had arrived, and they set about clearing new routes for the traffic in the neighbouring and still busy Argyle Street. There were many parked vehicles in the side streets and these had to be moved since they were obstructing the passage of fire appliances. That part of Anderston is very congested and the streets are narrow, but despite this, a fire tender with ladder and turntable was manoeuvered in front of the burning building, and another placed at the back of the warehouse in Warroch Street which, by this time, was completely engulfed in smoke. Firemen and police were issued with smoke equipment and by now dozens of hoses were pouring water on the conflagration. A large number of firemen were clustered around the tender in Cheapside Street preparing more hoses for use, when suddenly a blue flame appeared inside the burning building. The gases emitted by the heated alcohol exploded, blowing out the Cheapside wall of the building and collapsed the entire front on to the tender and firemen in the narrow street.

All available manpower on the scene, police and firemen, rushed to the smoking mountain of stone and rubble and tore at it with bare hands in an attempt to free the men trapped in the smouldering wreckage.

The tender had been buried to almost half its height by

the fallen masonry, and it was here that the rescuers concentrated their efforts to save anyone still alive. The majority of the rescuers were police, for almost the entire contingent of firemen in front of the warehouse had been buried by the collapsed wall. They worked ceaselessly throughout the night, pulling wounded men and dead bodies from under and around the half-buried tender. One policeman in particular, Constable T Gribbon, risked his own life time and time again, crawling amongst the rubble and the twisted remains of the fire turntable in an attempt to find survivors. On one of his forays into the wreckage he came across a wounded fireman trapped by the legs in a mass of bricks and twisted metal. With complete disregard for his own safety he was able to free the man. For this act of outstanding bravery officer Gribbon was awarded the BEM.

Nineteen firemen lost their lives in that tragedy and many others were severely injured.

On 2 of January 1971 Rangers were playing the traditional New Year's match against Celtic at home at Ibrox. The game was in its last minutes and Celtic was winning by one–nil. Hundreds of Rangers fans, resigned to their team's defeat, began to leave the stadium and streamed down stairway 13, a steep, broad, concrete staircase leading to the street below. Suddenly there was a roar from the crowd still inside the stadium. Rangers had scored, and the departing fans, suddenly elated at their team's unexpected reprieve, turned on the staircase in an attempt to re-enter the ground. They were met by a surge of people at the top of the stairs rushing to leave the ground. The two waves of people collided at the top of the staircase. Some stumbled and fell and were propelled backwards, to be engulfed in a mass of falling bodies, hurled back by the thousands now rushing to leave the stadium. Barriers gave way under the weight, body piled on body, and those in the middle were crushed.

The dozen or so police stationed in the street below were quick to realise what was happening and tried to urge those on the stairs to keep descending, but could hardly make themselves heard above the tumult and shrieks and cries of the injured and dying. Some seconds later the police at the top of the stairs also became aware of the unfolding tragedy and made an attempt to stop the rush towards the staircase. Some moments were to pass before a semblance of control could be established, but that control came far too late for the hundreds who lay in agony on the concrete steps. The police worked madly, pulling body away from body, trying to free the living from the dead, giving resuscitation to those in need, and helping to fill the ambulances which by now had arrived on the scene. That scene was one of indescribable horror. The dead lay six deep on the steps. The police worked incessantly until the last body had been recovered and until the last of the wounded had been seen to. Sixty-six people lost their lives in that tragedy and almost 200 suffered severe injuries. There is no doubt that had it not been for the prompt action of the police the toll would have been very much higher.

The Blackout

The blackout imposed in the towns and cities of the UK at the outbreak of war in 1939 created enormous problems, not only for the population in general, but for the police who patrolled the streets. In shops and houses, in factories and in all places of work, the blackout was total. No chink of light was permitted to escape from any premises. The windows of all houses and establishments were fitted with heavy, black curtains which had to be fully drawn at nightfall, with not a spark of light allowed to escape. The closes and landings of tenements remained unlit at night, and the streets were without any kind of illumination whatsoever. Any shop, restaurant or pub which catered to the public after dark had to take special precautions so that light would not spill out into the street as their doors were opened to permit entrance and exit. A sort of dark chamber had to be formed by the erection of two curtains, one flush on the street, and the other a few steps inside the premises, so that one had to be closed before the other was opened. These restrictions were very severely supervised, and woe betide anyone who allowed the slightest ray of light to escape from house or workplace. The police and the thousands of wardens from the newly created ARP corps kept a close look out for infringements, which could be punished by heavy fines, or in very extreme cases, by imprisonment.

The restrictions placed on vehicles were not as draconian, but were severe nevertheless. Although motor cars were far from numerous then, there were many transport motor vehicles on the road and these had to be allowed some form of illumination, not so much as to light up their route, but to give others warning of their presence. Headlight covers with narrow horizontal slits were fitted so that only the smallest ray of light would emerge, and this had to be slanted sharply downwards towards the road, giving practically no forward vision. The effect of all this on the daily life of the citizen was drastic. Daytime activities were practically untouched, but normal activity after dark was impossible and in the winter months, with darkness descending in the late afternoon, life in the city was almost at a standstill. Even at the best of times the atmosphere in Glasgow was heavily laden with coal smoke and in the winter this sometimes combined with fog to create a murky blackness. It was literally impossible to see your hand in front of your face and to drive a car or travel by bicycle in such circumstances was almost out of the question.

Almost, but not quite, for the main streets of Glasgow had built-in direction indicators, the tram lines, and it was a common sight to see vehicle after vehicle in single file following the tracks along some main street. The trams themselves were, of course, invaluable as a means of transport. They had no need of any form of lighting to see their way, they simply ran on their tracks no matter what the visibility, and Glasgow in wartime had cause to thank these slow and cumbersome means of transportation. In some places cart tracks served the same purpose as tramlines. Many Glagow streets had two parallel lines of smooth stone set into the cobbles for the use of horse drawn vehicles, and these too served as useful guides in the darkness.

In such conditions the work of the police was very difficult. Although the introduction of conscription had removed much of the adult criminal population from the streets, there were thousands of young hooligans not yet of military age to whom the blackout had come as a godsend. Under the cover of the all-pervading darkness they were able to roam the streets almost with impunity and no prudent citizen would venture outdoors after nightfall. Some did, however, and they were usually equipped with small hand torches, which gave the impression of disembodied lights floating in mid-air as their owners felt their way along the pavements.

Although many cinemas and places of entertainment closed early in the winter, most pubs and restaurants kept to their normal hours and catered as best they could for their reduced clientele. One of the pubs which kept to its normal routine was the famous 'Jock Mills' Variety Bar' situated at the top of West Nile Street, as it turned into the Cowcaddens. With its brightly decorated front, featuring the figure of a dancing clown painted on a vitrolite background, the pub was a very popular drinking place for the locals and for the visiting artistes appearing at nearby theatres. Inside it was bright, warm and enticing, in stark contrast to the world outside and every night it was well patronised by a regular clientele.

It was often patronised by the two policemen on the late shift, not for drinking purposes, for at closing time their shift still had an hour or so to run, but for a cup of tea and a break from the darkness and solitude of the streets. They were of help when the pub was closed up, a rather complicated procedure if no light was to be allowed to escape, what with the throwing of main light switches, the holding of curtains, the carrying of leather money bags and the locking of doors.

At the time in question, there had been no visit from the two constables for several days because of duties elsewhere, and the days of their absence had coincided with a period that four would-be thieves had kept the pub under surveillance.

For three consecutive nights these four young

criminals had watched from the dark street outside as the two charge hands closed up shop, emerged from the pub, leather bag in hand. They had caught a glimpse of the empty premises and had formulated a plan that they decided to put into action the very night that the two constables had taken up their old routine once more.

Unseen by the four would-be hold-up men, the two beat men had entered the pub by the back door about 15 minutes before closing, and were together with the two employees as they made their way out of the shop. One officer had been given the heavy leather cash bag to hold as one of the employees attended to the main light switch and, with the place now in darkness, the front door was unlocked, with the two policemen leading the way into the street. The door erupted into their faces. The four thieves charged it open, rushed in and slammed the door behind them, expecting to find two overcome, defenceless. However, they got the surprise and fright of their lives to find four people there instead of the two they had expected, and two of them very large policemen! In the pitch darkness of the pub a sudden sharp melee ensued, with shouts and oaths and imprecations interspersed with the sound of blows and the thud of fist and leather on flesh.

Suddenly the lights came on, switched on by one of the staff, to reveal a woeful sight. The four surprised and sorry hooligans lay spread-eagled on the floor, blood streaming from a variety of contusions, with one policeman nursing a bleeding nose. The thieves were handcuffed together, dragged to their feet, hustled unceremoniously to the nearby station and thrown into the cells. For days afterwards there was a certain coolness in the relationship between the two officers, for the one with the badly swollen nose swore his injury had been caused by the leather bag enthusiastically wielded by his neighbour during the fight!

✳   ✳   ✳

Not infrequently, on especially dark nights when all sense of orientation had gone, the pedestrian fumbling their uncertain way along the pavement could experience all kinds of weird sensations verging on panic, which on occasion could lead to strange results.

One night in November 1939, with the war just two months old, an elderly woman was gingerly feeling her way along Sauchiehall Street in an attempt to find the close of her flat in Elmbank Street, just round the corner from where she was groping her way along the pavement. The battery of her pencil torch had given out, she had lost all sense of direction and, completely disorientated, panic had begun to take over.

Coming slowly up behind her was the policeman on the beat, who was coping somewhat more successfully with the same difficulties. By this time the woman had become completely panic-stricken. All she could hear and see was the steady tramp of feet a few yards behind and the wavering beam of torchlight.

Convinced that she was about to be attacked, she stumbled and fell, shrieking at the top of her voice and lashed out with her handbag at the figure behind. The handbag caught the surprised constable on the side of the head, threw him momentarily off balance and caused him to drop his torch. He stooped to retrieve it and as he bent down hurriedly to fumble for it on the pavement he knocked himself unconscious against the metal of an unlit lamp-post. About 50 yards away another policeman was approaching from the opposite direction and he could clearly hear the sobbing and shrieking of a woman some distance ahead.

Convinced that an assault was taking place, he promptly blew his whistle to alert the distressed person to his presence and to summon assistance. This had the effect of alerting another policeman on the neighboring beat, who replied with a blast on his own whistle. A chain reaction was set off and soon the district was ringing with the blasts emitted by half a dozen Acme Thunderers, to which was added the whistle of the now conscious officer, who was convinced that he had been the victim of a gang attack. The pandemonium continued for a moment or so until the policemen ran out of breath and peace descended on the blacked-out streets once more.

Much of the following morning was devoted by the police to a search for the gang that had attacked one of their officers in the Elmbank Street–Sauchiehall Street area. Questions were asked of the housekeepers in the immediate district. One of those questioned was the the old woman's son, who had, after a fashion, witnessed the incident. He had gone into the street in search of his mother and had stumbled upon her just as the blow from her handbag set off the unfortunate chain of events. Prudence prevailed, however, and he thought it best to keep the truth of the matter to himself, leaving the incident to be written down in that day's report as an unsolved attack on a policeman.

Comparisons

In common with every other aspect of human activity, the manner in which the police operate in an attempt to maintain law and order in the community and to protect life and property has changed dramatically over the last 50 years.

The man on the beat has been relegated to the museum, along with his police box, Acme Thunderer and ten inch high helmet. Once upon a time he was an integral part of the community. He was known to all by name and he in turn knew every shopkeeper and the majority of the householders on his beat. His twice-daily stint on school crossings brought him into contact with families, while those escorted by him on the crossings grew to know him as a person to be trusted, respected and feared. He knew the good and the bad on his beat. His presence instilled a sense of security in the law-abiding citizen, and the fear of retribution and of punishment in the wrongdoer.

Today, this place has been taken by the impersonal police car and the ubiquitous eye of closed circuit television. It seems that society's perception of the police now is that of a remote figure, divorced from and only rarely seen in the neighbourhoods under their care. Now it seems that the police only appear on the scene as the result of a crime, the deterrent factor of their presence on the street is no longer there. The hooligan and the wrongdoer no longer fear and respect the police. A catalogue of restraints put upon the police by politicians in their dealing with the 'neds' has eliminated that fear and respect and has encouraged confrontation. In any clash with a criminal or wrongdoer the slightest hint of 'excessive' use of force by an officer makes the police the culprit and the criminal the victim, and the door is open for charges and claims of compensation to be made against them.

In an age of rapid technological advance and social change one does not expect the modus operandi of the police to remain as it was half a century ago. However, what the citizen is entitled to expect is that, in the same way that advances in medicine have dramatically lowered the incidence of disease in the community, modern methods of approach to the problem would have brought about, at the very least, the containment of crime in the community.

The reverse seems to be the case. One has only to look at the crime statistics over the past 50 years to see that the Glasgow of 50 years ago was a much safer place to live in than it is now. This is a list of crimes committed in Glasgow in three very separate years:

The statistics are from the Chief Constable's annual report for each year.

	1950	1960	1973
Crimes against the person	950	1,238	2,498
Crimes against property with violence	16,516	20,345	26,130
Crimes against property without violence	14,846	20,345	19,984
Malicious injury to property	1,842	123	659
Crimes against currency	110	172	219
Other crimes	267	401	807
Miscellaneous offences	24,017	55,485	67,977
Total crimes	58,548	93,185	117,253

In the ninteen ninties the categorisation of crime changed, as the following figures for the year 1996 show. The incidence of crime is ever upward:

Crimes of violence against the person (non-sexual)	6,953
Crimes involving indecency	1,618
Crimes involving dishonesty	69,312
Fireraising, malicious and reckless conduct	16,961
Other crimes	19,700
Miscellaneous offences	29,789
Total crimes	144,333
Motor vehicle offences	51,284
Total crimes and offences	195,615

Even by discounting the 51,000 motoring offences and bearing in mind that the population of Glasgow has diminished by one third in the last 40 years, it would seem from the above figures that the city, for whatever reason, is a much more dangerous place to live in now than it was then.

One statistic from the year 1989 for the whole of the Strathclyde area is staggering. In that year there were 30 attempted murders of police officers in the region. In the same year there were also 2,959 assaults on police personnel.

This inexorable rise of crime in the community is of course due to many complex factors, but it seems that to some extent it is caused by the constraints put on the forces of law and order by the wave of politically correct social tinkering which permeates all western societies. The criminal is held not to be responsible for their actions, but it is society which makes the criminal, goes the thought of the day. The wrongdoer has to be analysed, understood and counselled rather than disciplined and constrained. The police officer dare not lay a heavy hand on the hooligan or they will be accused of brutality and placed in the dock themselves. The citizen dare not protect themselves or their property vigorously lest they are charged with an offence, the teacher dare not chastise an unruly pupil lest they are charged with an assault. Sentences passed on criminals are often derisory and bear no relationship to the crime committed. A householder in England has recently been sentenced to life imprisonment for the killing of a burglar on his premises, no different from the sentence that would have been passed on Manuel had he been tried today for his multiple murders, or on Bible John should he ever be caught.

The concept of discipline and personal responsibility seems to have vanished from society. Responsibility is deemed to lie elsewhere; shamed and discredited politicians no longer resign, blame is seldom accepted, compensation is sought from somewhere or someone for the slightest personal misfortune or inconvenience and everyone seems to talk of 'rights' but never of 'duty'. On his retirement in May 1977, Deputy Chief Constable Elphinstone Dalglish, whose contribution to the police in solving murders and serious crimes during his period of service dating from 1936 is second to none, (in an interview on 25 May 1977 in the *Evening Times*) made the statement that violence was the single greatest problem facing police in the west of Scotland. 'People's living standards and social conditions have improved greatly in the past 30 years,' he said, 'but there is no sign of any betterment in the violent behaviour of some. I see a strong police force as being absolutely essential to an ordered life.'

The above statement is even more valid today. A report published by Strathclyde Police at the end of February 2000 states that, in one district alone, seven out of ten children aged between 14 and 15 had committed a crime in the previous year. Police officers from specialised units and hundreds of uniformed officers raided 2,506 licensed premises, where 25% of violent crime takes place. In them 40 persons, some of them children, were arrested. In the month of February alone, more than 500 persons were arrested for violent crime or for carrying weapons. The need for political action in the support of an efficient and resolute police force is obviously greater now than it ever was before.

The Police Museum

Much of the historical material contained in this book has been gathered from the Glasgow Police Museum in Pitt Street. The museum, housed unobtrusively in the basement of the Strathclyde Police Headquarters building, is cared for by the Assistant Curator, May Mitchell, a former police officer. Inaugurated on 3 August 1990, the museum houses a unique collection of police memorabilia of the 200 years of the Glasgow police and can be visited by members of the public by prior arrangement. It consists of scores of well laid out exhibits which depict the growth of the Glasgow police from its simple beginnings in the eighteenth and nineteenth centuries. It also documents the merger of the Glasgow police force with other Scottish forces, creating the new Strathclyde force in 1975. This force is now the second largest in the nation, second in size to the Metropolitan in London.

The Strathclyde region encompasses more than 2,000,000 people, almost half the population of Scotland, and takes in an area stretching from the mountains of Glencoe in the north to Ayrshire in the south, and from the inner Hebrides in the west to East Lanarkshire. The Strathclyde police force employs 7,200 officers in active police duty and also 2,000 civilians, known as Force Support Personnel, in auxiliary roles.

The museum's exhibits are attractively and clearly arranged in historical sequence, beginning with a display of paintings and photographs of the Chief Constables of the Glasgow police. The emphasis is on Sir James Smart, the first with the title of Chief Constable of Glasgow conferred on him in 1862, on Sir Percy Sillitoe, whose appointment to the post in 1931 heralded a period of change and innovation for the Glasgow police and then on Sir David McNee, the last Chief Constable of Glasgow and the first of the new Strathclyde region.

There are a series of displays depicting the evolution of the force from its beginnings in June 1800, when it received official recognition by the granting of a Royal assent. The evolution of the uniform, from the cumbersome greatcoat of the early 'watchmen', as they were named, to the one familiar to us now, is there, together with examples of early police equipment, such as the rattles and wooden clappers used as a means of communication by the men on the beat. The phrase 'run like the clappers' used by hooligans to spur one another on in running away from the police probably stems from the use of these. The clappers and rattles eventually gave way to the famous 'Acme Thunderer' whistle, which survived until the arrival of the two-way radio in the early sixties.

Also on show are the types of baton used throughout the years, as well as the cutlasses used by the Calton Burgh force prior to its incorporation into the Glasgow district. In addition to their principle duty of keeping the peace during night hours, the early watchmen served as leeries and street sweepers and the equipment used by them is displayed. Policemen on horses first appeared on the streets in 1924 and in this section there is a life-like figure of the first mounted policeman in an imposing military-style uniform complete with ornamental sabre.

Early techniques used in the identification of criminals are demonstrated. These entailed the use of ingeniously mirrored photographs to show frontal and profile images simultaneously. The facial image was accompanied by a photograph of the hands, a technique which predated modern fingerprinting procedures.

The forgery display shows the clever methods used in counterfeiting banknotes, with examples of 'note splitting', a procedure whereby a banknote was expertly split in two,

177

thereby effectively doubling the value of your money if anyone was gullible enough to accept the split note.

Some of the most notorious murders in Glasgow of the twentieth century are dealt with, an emphasis being put on the Oscar Slater case and the savage Manuel murders. The Slater case has gone into history as one of the most ignoble miscarriages of justice ever. The display contains a detailed account of the case and a facsimile of the eventual exoneration of the policeman Trench who had been determind to see justice done. There are also accounts and exhibits from the Allison Street shootings of 1969 (recounted here in chapter eight) and of the Charles Street robbery of 1973.

The Peter Manuel murders are graphically portrayed. The long catalogue of murders for which he was executed was horrific, and they still shock, even in an age sated with reports of multiple murders. His trial came as grist to the mill of the tabloid press who were supplied day after day with sensational stories about the casual traffic in guns in various Glasgow pubs, of illegal and violent gambling schools on the banks of the Clyde and of petty criminals running errands in and out of Barlinnie for shadowy crime bosses.

During his long trial he saw fit to dismiss his counsel and conducted his own defence with a certain degree of skill, but at the end of it all he was found guilty of the murder of eight victims. He was also wanted in Newcastle for the murder of a taxi driver and whilst in prison awaiting execution he confessed to the murder of three more, making a total of twelve persons killed by him.

He was hanged in July 1958 in Barlinnie prison, the last but one to be executed there. That dubious distinction belongs to Anthony Millar, aged 19, who was executed in the Barlinnie hanging shed in December 1960. The hanging shed at Barlinnie was demolished in 1995 and the occasion was marked by an article in the *Herald* by Leonard Murray, the solicitor who had defended Millar at his trial. The exhibit also displays an array of guns and other weapons used in Manuel's dreadful career, together with a detailed account of his crimes.

Prominently featured is the police sporting cabinet, with a display of trophies won by the Glasgow police over the years. Pride of place is given to a photograph of the 1889 tug-of-war team taken on the occasion of their victory at a tournament in Paris. The average height of the team is six foot two inches and their Captain is a William McIntosh, said to be the father of the famous Charles Rennie McIntosh.

The forensic sciences are well displayed with detailed examples and explanations of their application in crime detection, and this section is followed by the 'drugs cabinet'. On exhibition are some of the scales confiscated in drugs raids and a range of coins used as counterweights for the weighing of drugs by pushers and addicts.

We are shown how fingerprints are taken and comparison is made between modern methods of matching them by computer with the slow and man-power consuming methods used in earlier days. Close by can be seen a remarkable relic saved for the museum from the old Govan police station by May Mitchell herself. On the closure of that station the furnishings were examined with a view to keeping something of interest for the museum, and the item chosen was the Govan muster-room door. It dates from 1867 and stands an imposing seven foot three inches from floor level to underside of lintel, the height necessary to accommodate the possible six foot four inches height of a constable plus the ten or so extra inches of his helmet.

A birch and birching board used in the whipping of male offenders is on show. The weight of the birches varied according to the age of the recipient, the lightest of them being reserved for offenders of eight, the earliest age at which birching could be prescribed as a punishment.

Then comes a section on the notorious Glasgow gangs and the fearsome array of lethal weapons used by them. Knuckledusters, knives of all shapes and sizes, razors, bicycle chains, spiked clubs, bayonets, all these and more are on show, giving a slight idea of how vicious these gang fights were and unfortunately still are. The exhibits on show are from the amnesty declared in Easterhouse on the occasion of the entertainer Frankie Vaughn's campaign to bring youth occupational programmes to the area in the sixties.

Towards the end of the tour, a section is devoted to the activities of the police during the times of blackout and bombing in last war. Finally there is an original police pillar box, of the type introduced by Percy Sillitoe in 1933 and kept in use in some parts of the city until the sixties. The official title is 'Police Pillar Telephone System' and it consists of a cast-iron vandalproof lighthouse-like structure with a mesh-protected light on top. At the end of the display there is perhaps the most impressive and poignant display of all: three commemorative glass showcases dedicated to police officers killed in the line of duty.

Joe Beattie

Joe Beattie, one of the finest of 'The Big Men', sadly passed away on 10 February, 2000. His was a meteoric career which started in 1946 as a constable and during which he rose to the rank of detective superintendent. Some of his recollections have contributed to passages in this book.

This eulogy was spoken at his funeral by Leonard Murray, the noted Glasgow solicitor.

Eulogy to Joe Beattie

Joan and the family have honoured me by asking me to say a few words about Joe. But how can any mere words pay sufficient tribute to that fine, brave man.

Joe and I went back a long way – to the days when I was still at school and he and Joannie were neighbours of my sister. He was the big polis up the stairs just out of the RAF who had married the lovely English girl.

We met up again when I qualified and Joe took me under his wing and brought me into that huge circle of people who were his friends and for whom he would do anything he could. And we all owe a great deal to Joe Beattie; and my family and I will always be grateful to him for the help, the encouragement and above all the friendship, which we enjoyed at his hands for forty-odd years.

An enormous number of people owe much to Joe and to what he did for them. It was not for any thanks that he did it but out of a deep sense of caring and compassion for others.

He had outstanding success in his chosen career both in the CID and in uniform, and he was one of that tiny elite corps, the finest police officers that I have ever been privileged to know.

And he enjoyed enormous respect, from his colleagues, from the press, from my profession, from the Bench and even from the very people that he locked up. I never heard a bad word about Joe from any one of them.

And that perhaps was the measure of the man, he gained respect wherever he went.

For a whole generation he was much more than just a polis from Maitland Street. Before community policing was ever invented Joe was a community policeman: he was a counsellor before the word counselling was ever discovered; for he was an institution.

In his latter years he suffered greatly and indeed it was miraculous that he survived so long. But he could not have survived without the unfailing love and devotion of Joannie who nursed him so tenderly for so long. And in all of those years of serious illness his bravery and his fighting spirit were inspiring.

Joe was not a church-going man but listen to these words:

Whatever mitigates the woes or increases the happiness of others, this is my criterion of goodness; but whatever injures society at large or any individual in it, then this is my measure of iniquity.

God knows I'm no saint, but if I could, and I believe that I do it as far as I can, I would wipe all tears from all eyes.

Those words the very quintessence of Christian love, were written by Robert Burns but they could have been written by Joe Beattie.

In my own Church the Requiem Mass contains a sentence which is so fundamental to Christian belief:

Lord, for your faithful people life is changed, not ended.

With the passing of Joe Beattie life is changed. It is changed for all who knew him for they have lost one whom they respected and admired; it is changed for those of us privileged to be called his friends for we have lost someone very special; but above all it is changed for Joannie, Sandra and Anne, and all the family, a family of whom he was so proud, for they have lost someone who loved them very dearly and to whom they were everything.

A mould has been broken. An era has ended, and life has changed for everyone of us whose lives were touched by this lovely man.

But this is not an occasion for us just to shed a selfish tear at our loss. It is also an occasion for thanking God, not just for having created such a wonderful character, but also for having extended to us the privilege and the honour of his friendship.For each and every one of us who knew Joe Beattie is the better and the richer for the experience.

There is an old Arab proverb which says that the best legacies a man can leave are good memories and Joe has left an abundance of good memories to us all.

It is in the Gospel of St Matthew that we read: 'Well done good and faithful servant; enter into the joy of your Master.'

On Thursday of last week Joe Beattie entered into that joy, and his pain and his suffering are no more.

Leonard G. Murray
16 February 2000